MW01104070

rebels

of

grace

the passionate life of
freedom in god

by aaron currin

TATE PUBLISHING, LLC

To my brother Nate, whose journey has revealed to me more of the stunning portrait of God's grace. Living on as rebels...

Recommendation from Young Readers

"Rebels of Grace reveals the wonderful freedom and awesome responsibility that Christ's death and resurrection brings to us. It will be both an immense comfort and a great challenge to its readers."
—Tim Sinclair, student majoring in biblical studies at Covenant College

"Simply incredible! A beautiful portrayal of grace that leaves the reader very much aware of God's indescribable love and our response to that love!"
—Jessica Adams, student majoring in cross-cultural communications at the University of Florida

"One of the clearest descriptions of grace I have ever come across! The truth of this book will transform the way young people view religion and Christianity! Rebels of Grace is a must read for every young follower of Christ!"
—Becky D. Adams, former Theology student and current youth worker in Illinois

"Though Aaron's writing is extremely easy to understand, it remains incredibly deep, delving into the mystery of grace. His explanation of mercy as the catalyst to a God-centered life reshaped my priorities as I realized that I can glorify God in all I do!"
—Cory Crane, student majoring in business management at the University of West Florida

Contents

1

a call to *rebel*

See to it that no one takes you captive by
philosophy and empty deceit, according to human
tradition, according to the elemental spirits of
the world, and not according to Christ.

Colossians 2:8

Pensacola, Florida—February 2004
"C'mon Bible college—don't fail me now!"

My posture would have never betrayed my anxiety.
Slouched over on one of those cheaply constructed cafe
chairs, my chin rested on the arch of the seat-back. My
eyes placidly studied the tiled floor. A small sigh escaped
my lips. Sure, I may have appeared the picture of relaxation, even boredom, yet inside my mind was desperately
racing.

Across from me sat a 16-year-old girl. Tears spilt from
reddened eyes. Glossy trails coursed across the young

cheeks. She had trouble meeting my gaze, and when she did, I found my own eyes uneasily darting away. The Bible study, I helped to lead at my home church, had ended what seemed like hours ago. The weekly youth get-to-gether following our study, which typically consisted of burgers and ice cream, had concluded. Now each teen was on his or her way home. Thoughts filled the young minds—school the following morning, a dreaded work-place, or the "need" for a romantic companion in his or her ever-changing, adolescent life. All thoughts curious-ly roamed elsewhere, except for that of this particular young woman.

Tough situations...problems in her family...intense depression...This teenager was at the end of her emo-tional rope. Life was a miserable hole of letdowns and complexities. Her mind whirled as she vainly attempted to understand the circumstances of the tiny picture that was her life and how it somehow fit into the magnificent portrait that is the story of God. Part of her wanted to pursue her relationship with Him—wanted to jump into a passionate love-life with her Savior—but she felt unwor-thy. Sure, she had prayed a prayer—asked Jesus into her life—but still because of personal failures and unbelief, she felt rejected.

"When I do good things I feel like God is smiling at me, but for the most part, like now, I feel like I can't measure up, and therefore, He's frowning and stands miles away."

This single phrase hung in the air like a sickening cloud of black smoke. It caught me off guard, made my head spin. My mind whirled trying to conjure up a good one-liner to settle the roaring emotions of this dejected young woman.

However, all the catchy Sunday school clichés and theological courses at Bible college seemed extremely pithy or practically useless on this particular evening. The girl before me had heard the run-of-the-mill orthodox counsel before. She had read the books on "how to get the most out of the Christian life" and strolled through the "making God happy" devotionals. She had been screamed at by red-faced dogmatists, declaring to her that it was her duty to please God. She had felt hands patting her on the back and heard voices telling her she just had unbalanced hormones, as hands shoved pills in her face. And now she sat facing me, head hung low, having stated what many young adults and teens of today feel to be true—overwhelming pressure from a Divine bully who with arms crossed glares down from Heaven almost taking pleasure in the fact that we are not as holy as we ought to be!

Perhaps you are on the same ride with my young friend. You, too, feel unworthy. You, too, feel that God is distant and that He is angry with you because you slipped up or because you are always slipping up. Maybe you feel the need to satisfy your craving by dipping a foot—or maybe just a toe—into the passionless vile of this world. Or maybe, just maybe, you are sick of it all—nauseated by mindless traditions, tired of what the 21st-century church, a best selling paperback, or some well-meaning youth leader *tells* you is truth. You are disgusted by the stereo-typical, hypocritical Christian of today.

Young person, DON'T throw off this life called Christianity! DON'T give into the pressures of the god of philosophy, entertainment, or sex! And though you might be revolted by the hypocrisy of modern Christianity and the age-old traditions of God-professing "believers," please DON'T forsake the God of this universe simply because certain people or groups who claim to know Him are more concerned with promoting their believable lies than holding to His incredible truth! DON'T be just another casualty!

We do not need more young people who say they believe in God, yet claim that everyone in the church is hypocritical. There is no more room for the spiritually apathetic, the worldly minded, or the religiously proud! The time has come to abandon all that is traditional, to cast off the philosophies of "intellectuals," and to drown the damning comfort of lifeless Christianity!

Now is the time to discover who God really is! Time to understand what grace truly does!

Young friend, it is time to start a rebellion!

That's what we need in this time of godless, self-satisfying Christians. It seems that college students I encounter are merely conforming to who they "feel" God is. Teenagers are looking for acceptance in the new idea, philosophy, or fad to burst onto the scene. And the Bible—the very breath of God Himself—is now, to many young people, simply an out-dated manuscript of archaic ideas and laughable commands.

Many are slipping into lifeless ideologies about "god." They believe what has the *appearance* of truth—their spiritual equilibrium established and maintained by what the parents have drilled into them or what the pastor states on Sunday morning. Every theory they possess about Jesus Christ has been molded by a history book, an intellectual fellow student, or their own depraved rationalization. Each concept they have of the Holy Spirit is crafted by what believers of today hail as "worship." Young people either feel that they are pleasing their Lord because *they* have sacrificed and served enough (please don't miss the emphasis on "they"), or young people, such as my young friend in the fast food restaurant, suffer under the agonizing realization that they can never measure up and be "holy" enough to please God.

The rest of this generation simply tumbles into the darkened mindset that God is cold and disconnected (though they might never actually state this), and these teenagers/young adults become far more committed to the opinions of man than the Word of God. Though many of these so-called believers allege to be Christians, frequent the youth group or college gatherings, have moments of expressive praise, or talk about how "amazing God is!" the reality of a Savior from sin is a completely foreign concept. Though the existence of a Creator is acknowledged from these lips, the lifestyles of these same young men and women prove that they are actually practical atheists (those who deny the reality of God)! Why? Because we (not just the youth I am speaking of, but you and I as well) often live our lives as if God Himself does not truly exist.

None of the ideas above portrays the One who Scripture calls I AM! None of them turn our eyes from meaningless clods of dirt (yea, you and I again), to the God who is EVERYTHING! None of them teaches us of ruthless, agonizing love and the reaction to true freedom!

aaron *carrin*

And this is why I now am calling for this rebellion! This is what Paul cried for the Colossian church: "Don't let anyone imprison you in the chains of empty philosophical deceit, which comes from human traditions and mindless, worldly idolatry ..." Don't let television, the music industry, a best-selling author, friends, family, books, or even the teachings of the church (if they are not Word-centered) lead you into a dark cell, slamming the door behind you! Traditions of men and women—regardless of their intellect—and the way of this world's system of thinking will only mold you into a rebel *against* grace! Our primary intent is not to rebel against worldly philosophy or religious tradition though. Rather, as it were, our aim is to be chained to Christ! The most liberating freedom in the world is slavery to Jesus Christ (Col. 2:8b)!

We are to be rebels *of* grace! Your focus, as well as mine, should not be on what we are rebelling against but rather on what our cause for rebellion is! It is *His* grace—God's grace. We must become captivated in HIM!

Our young lives must be saturated by a proper and practical understanding of extreme grace!

The design of this book is not to assist *you* in accepting *yourself,* help *you* to discover *your* purpose, or transform *you* into the all-conquering super Christian! It is rather to reverse the spotlight so that the light swings away from you and I to once again illuminate the Person of Christ Jesus before our eyes of clay! And then as we see Him as He should be seen, and as His work of grace blazes forth in as much of its glory as we can swallow...

we will hopefully rise together and shout as one, "*Let us live as rebels of grace!*"

Young person, it's time to spark a rebellion.

2

Forgiven!

God has purchased our freedom with His
blood and has forgiven all our sins.
Colossians 1:13a, 14 NLT

Jerusalem, 28 a.d.

The heat of the afternoon sun is sweltering. Women fan their perspiring brows, attempting to find some relief. Sweat-soaked children chase diseased dogs through the streets. An old carpenter sits on the steps of his wood shop, gazing out at passersby. Grown men push hastily by with a slight nod or a barely discernable smile behind wooly beards. It had been a lazy afternoon and fairly un-eventful...but the shouts bring the tedious boredom to an abrupt end.

Every eye along the thoroughfare turns toward the cries. Shopkeepers gather in their doorways to witness the cause for commotion. Even the children pause for an instant and the fans of the women halt, poised in mid-air.

The crowd appears. Those leading the mob are clearly recognizable to the average observer. They wear the traditional attire of religious rulers; they are obviously very angry. Stumbling from the throng, a young woman falls into the dust of the street. The religious rulers grab at her hair and tattered dress. Yanking her painfully to her feet, they push her forward. She stumbles, almost falling facefirst into chalky dirt once more. She attempts to right herself but another rough hand shoves her in the back and once more she is thrown off balance. Tears streak her cheeks. Her face is shrouded in fear and embarrassment. Staggering down a narrow stairway she tries to avoid trouncing on the long robes sweeping just inches before her soiled feet. At the base of the flight of stone steps, she trips. Arms flailing, she collapses in a heap. Her knees are now bloodied. Her hands scrape the stone-covered ground; her dress is shredded further. Sobs wrack her chest—which seems to be burdened with an enormous load of inexplicable weight. The rough hands jerk her back to her feet, and half walking-half crawling, the woman continues her anxious trek.

Where were they taking her? She had already resigned herself to the fate she was sure would come...but why had they not carried it out already? Her crime was looked upon as one of the most heinous transgressions a soul could commit. These—her oppressors—had caught her in the act of satisfying her sexual desires with a man that was not her husband. Therefore, she was certain that death would be her punishment. The woman wonders now if her husband has been informed of his wife's wickedness but is too humiliated to come out to witness the execution. She could try to pin her unfaithfulness on him—perhaps he was not the husband he should have been or he did not fulfill her passions or he himself had been involved in adulterous affairs. None of these mental accusations, though, excused the vile and immoral behavior of this young woman.

She would never forget being in the very act of her sensuous pleasure with her lover when the doors burst open and filling the doorway were several of the very prominent religious leaders of the city. Now her sin—which she had felt tinges of guilt over before—seemed monstrous to her. After all, these holy men had now seen what *she was sure* they had never even *thought* of! The Pharisees and the scribes were righteous; some thought that these men never transgressed the law in idea or action. Therefore, to be caught as an adulteress, and to now feel the wrath of these men searing at her conscience, was more than she could bear. How much further must they go? Could they not just execute her now and be done with it? Her feelings of degradation would be dead with her body, and the wrath of the leaders would be appeased.

As the procession of the holy men and this one, lone woman makes its way down the streets, the scribes call to other religious men to join the convoy. The woman holds her head low in bitter grief as snarling insults bombard her ears. She does hear the Pharisees cry out to other comrades that they were going to *test* the "blasphemer," though the statements do not particularly pique her interest. For all she knew, she might be the very blasphemer of whom they spoke. Enthralled with the parade and pleased that the attention was focused on the adulteress's sins, and thus averted from their own, men run to join the march. By the time the crowds reach their destination, the numbers of her accusers have drastically increased.

It does not occur to the woman that her journey is complete, until she rounds a corner and feels another terrific heave in her lower back! The momentum drives her through the Pharisees walking before her. Her wrists once again slam into the ground and she winces painfully. A sharp stone scrapes across her cheek, marring the once-lovely face. Fresh-mud, made from her flowing tears, soils her forehead. Features mashed into the dirt, she feels as if she can cry no more. Her *condemnation* is inconceivable! She knows she deserves to die, and at this moment, death would be a welcome relief. Existence for her is only one on-going, excruciating torment.

Finding herself to be in a small courtyard of sorts, the realization finally comes to her that these are the grounds just outside the temple—the *most* holy place. So they had brought her here for the execution, perhaps as an example. She half expects to feel the blow of a stone against the back of her skull, but no stones come.

From her peripheral vision she detects a crowd to her right hand side. She is well aware that her accusers are just a few steps behind her, but she senses a peculiar presence looking down from directly before her. Through the tresses of her tangled black curls and the haze of her own tears, she slowly lifts her gaze. She squints to focus on the sight that fills her vision.

There stands a Man. His eyes are piercing, as if He can see right through her. In those eyes shine a radiant splendor that conveys, could it be, *hope?* His clothes are plain. From her fallen position she can see the Hebrew sandals on his calloused feet. The hardened clay on His sandals and toes attests to the fact that He is a traveler. There is certainly nothing flashy or handsome about His external appearance. A thick beard shrouds His cheeks and partially covers His upper lip. His olive-toned skin is dark from constant exposure to the sun. He does not speak right away upon the intrusion. Instead, He carefully evaluates the situation, as if estimating the severity of the situation before an indictment can even be hurled.

Upon seeing that the Man before the adulteress was not going to utter a word until an explanation was given as to this interruption, one of the Pharisees steps forward. "Look, Teacher, this woman here," his bony finger accusingly protrudes from the wool robe, "has been caught in the very act of sex with a man other than her husband!" As if on cue, a gasp arises from the crowd of onlookers. Allowing his declaration to settle and the throng to grow still once more, the religious leader pauses for a moment before continuing.

For some reason, the fallen adulteress begins to feel her sorrow altering. Before hand, the capture at the hands of the rulers and the condemnation she knew would come, sickened her. Now however, upon coming face-to-face with this Man—this Man who exudes not the false, outward holiness of the Pharisees, but a genuine, inner, righteous peace—she begins to feel the enormous weight of her wickedness before Jehovah God. With all other emotions fading, the woman begins to discern the true gravity of her sin as her eyes fix upon the face of this solitary traveler.

The Pharisee's voice echoes against the temple walls. "Now in the just law of Moses, the commandment is that this woman should be stoned to death!" Another pause. Then the query falls: "So what do *you* say we should do?"

The young woman is beginning to feel as if her trial is no longer the primary issue of concern. It is as if she is merely a pawn in a much larger chess game, and the Pharisees are more than willing to sacrifice her to win this battle. The sin she had committed was somehow being twisted in an attempt to trip up and indict this strange Man before her. *Blasphemer?* Could this be the One of whom they spoke? *A test...*Perhaps this Man was the blasphemer that was to be tried. But why?

With barely controllable emotions dangerously close to spilling over, the captive woman watches as the Traveler slowly bends His knees, lowering Himself to a crouched position. With the tip of His index finger He outlines something in the sand. His hands are rugged, no doubt from a lifetime of physical labor. The woman gazes not to the sand, but instead to the peaceful features of this Man. What thoughts fill the mind of the One they call, "Teacher"? The crowd is silent; the atmosphere is somehow growing tranquil, but the leaders become impatient. How could He simply doodle in the soil when the life of this young woman hangs in the balance?

"Come now, Teacher. What is your answer?" one demands abruptly.

Slowly, He rises to His feet. His eyes pierce the hearts of the antagonists. His words sear the accusations in their spirits.

"Whoever here has never sinned...that Man...can throw the first stone at her."

His gaze meets the gaze of each accuser. None are able to hold it. Moments tick away. Once more the bearded Man of meekness stoops down to that crouched position and continues the outline in the dusty soil.

Thunk.

Every eye in the crowd darts to the oldest and most prominent of the religious leaders, and then to the rock which now creates tiny cyclones of dust at his feet. He turns and staggers away, as if stunned by the words that had just been declared. It is not long before the next man deliberately turns as well, followed by another and then another. Finally, each accuser vanishes. For each accuser and each person who had let out a shocked gasp, the oldest man to the youngest child, is guilty!

Who is this Man? The mind of the woman whirls. *Could this be the great Teacher of whom I have heard so much? Could this be the Galilean?* Glancing once more to where her captors had stood, she feels like exploding into a dance of joy! Instead, with eyes still fixed on the traveler, she cautiously erects herself to a standing position. Her soiled fingers rise to brush a tear from her cheekbone as she marvels at the Man who had lifted the condemnation from her shoulders and transferred it to the hearts of her very accusers.

After moments of silence the bearded Man places both hands on his knees, pushing Himself upward. His words are not laced in censure as they had been with the religious scribes and Pharisees, rather compassion flows in His voice. "Woman, where are your accusers? Didn't even one of them condemn you?" Though the inquiry concerned her captors, the Man does not glance about to see where these men had gone. His eyes penetrate hers.

Peace is conveyed without further words. It is as if His query had been rhetorical, to simply demonstrate that all men and women are vile in thought or action, or both. Not one of her accusers had been able to stand against the straightforward remark from the lips of this bearded Teacher. All of them were wicked. And therefore, this Man had established the truth that *every* person—not just this detestable adulteress—was in desperate need of forgiveness and reconciliation to a truly, holy God.

Nervously, the young woman sweeps a black strand away from her dark eyes. It finally dawns upon her whom she is addressing. He is...He is...She can't help but smile now. Her reply to His question is slightly hesitant. "No one, Lord."

A slim smile of triumph turns the lips of the Traveler upward. With a slight shake of His head, he speaks once more:

"Neither do I condemn you...but now go...and leave your life of sinfulness!"

In a state of total ecstasy and liberated bliss, the forgiven adulteress raises both hands heavenward, falling to her knees! Fresh tears parade unchecked, forming clear trails across the filthy, bloodied cheeks. Crawling rapidly to His side, she kisses the traveled feet of her Savior. The hand, which would one day take a Roman spike, reaches out to gently touch her head. The forgiveness of this Man, the Son of God Himself, is too much for her weary mind to take in. All she can murmur in response, over and over again, is "Thank you, thank you so much!"

3

Bury the *lies*

For by a single offering He has perfected for all time
those who are being sanctified! Hebrews 10:14

So what do you think?

After this mind-blowing, life-altering moment of exoneration, do you really believe that the forgiven girl would simply fall into line with the religious customs of the overly-traditional Pharisees? Or do you feel that after complete amnesty from the repercussions of her sin that she would put off the warped appetites of sexual passion only momentarily before ultimately returning to the very thoughts and acts she had been forgiven of? Or do you, in that frozen capsule of time (as she is completely pardoned from her transgressions) believe that she could possibly be focused on how *she could earn* the approval of her new found Lord?

To all of these conclusions the answer is NO! She

would not conform to the comatose traditions of the "religious." Nor would she slip backwards into the same sin she had been ransomed from. And realizing that the forgiveness she had received had nothing to do with her merit of it—for she had not even asked for it—surely she would not turn now to a wage for work-based relationship with God.

Instead, no doubt, she became a rebel!

She would revolt against the "holier than all" mindset of the Pharisees. She would war against sin, as a mutineer to the world's schemes because she understood and had experienced grace. Friend, the grace of the first century a.d. is the same grace we must find in the 21st century of today!

What is grace? It is God demonstrating how majestic He is by choosing to pour out the merits of His Son on sinners (you and me) so that we now have the desire and ability to grasp the eternal value of His glory and live for that glory. Simply put, grace is the undeserved smile of God. Scripture declares that we are all brought into God's family by this grace alone (Eph. 2:8–9). Yet though we are saved by grace that we did not earn, we so often try to merit the continued goodwill of God by performing "righteous" deeds. I begin to believe that my walk with God is dependant upon *my* performance. As long as I keep a clean nose, read my Bible once in a 24-hour period, and try to live a "holy" lifestyle, God will continue to look down on me and smile with approving love. As soon as I sin, however, I am in deep trouble. Oh sure, God still loves me, but He doesn't look at me the same as before. For the time being, I am distant from God, having forfeited His good favor because of my evil thoughts or actions.

I have observed in traveling and working with believers, young and old, that we have all fallen prey to looking at the Christian life in this way:

Saved by grace—gain God's daily favor through my works.

Now before you say "No way!" to this allegation, stop for a moment and think. You are a young man; you're surfing the net when you run across a pornographic site. For a time you feed your lustful imaginations. Finally, in a fit of conviction you click the "X" button at the top of the screen and begin confessing. Having confessed your sin before God, you are still reeling from the effects of it when the phone rings. On the other line is a young friend who needs prayer for a tough time he is going through. Do you immediately feel a sense of dread settle upon you? Do you feel "unworthy" to enter into God's presence and cry out to Him for direction in the life of your young comrade? If this is the case, you do not honestly understand the work of Christ on the cross, and you are still living on the basis of your works and not on His grace.

You're a young woman. It is a sunny Saturday, and you could do any number of things. However, you decide to spend the morning and early afternoon passing out tracts in the park or going from house to house with your Bible in hand sharing Christ with neighbors. After hours of witnessing with great results (or zero response) you walk into your house, feel the cool AC hit you in the face, and sink into the recliner. Do you at that moment feel as if God's smile upon you is growing? Do you imagine that He is going to bless you so abundantly or answer your prayers because you sacrificed for Him? If that is your response to a day of selfless serving, then you are living on the basis of your works and not on His grace.

Come on, we can admit it. Is this not how we all think and behave at times? I just had a sexual thought, made a perverted comment, lied about my test results, cursed at my parents...now there is no way that I can talk to God or instruct anyone on how to find peace with Him or partici-pate in worship. After all, I am unworthy! Why is this? The answer is simply that we don't see grace and the favor of God as a truly free and unmerited gift! While we would say that we are saved by God's wonderful grace, we would have to admit—with these notions in mind—that we are living a "Christian life" that bears striking similarities to a gold-star/demerit kindergarten class. When we do what's right, we get Divine, golden stickers; when we mess up, we get a black "D" by our names and a scowl of contempt from the face of God. We have twisted the truth, and now—though we would claim that we are still living by grace—we are actually walking a road of spiritual defeat based on our own efforts. We feel that as long as we are trying hard enough to maintain our spiritual walk then God is pleased with us. But one screw up...one day of failing to talk to Him or spending time in His Book....Well, yea, He is hacked off.

Young friend, this is not grace! This is a lie!

Are you saying I should cover my sin and then not feel the weight of hypocrisy, Aaron? Absolutely not, friend. Am I communicating that God shows us favor based on the *wicked* acts we commit? No way. Sin is an affront to God. It is outright rebellion against Christ. If you decide to live in sin this simply proves that you have never truly experienced genuine salvation (1 John 3:9). My message is for those who *have* tasted of grace...and it is a message that boldly cries out that you will never suffer the condemnation of God! You are free! You are righteous! And though you may stumble, and grieve the Spirit of God, His smile will never fade and His love will always remain the same (Rom. 8:38–39).

Are you saying that I shouldn't tell others about Christ, Aaron? Once more, absolutely not! What I am stating though is that God does not bestow favor and love upon us because of good deeds. Grace is not based upon a merit system. Listen carefully to this statement, my friend, for it may very well change your Christian life:

God loves you, favors you, and blesses you not because of the things you do or don't do, but because of what Jesus Christ has done for you!

Therefore, God shows us favor *in spite* of the wicked—or the righteous—acts we commit!

What liberation is found in this truth!

Grace is not something we merely need for salvation to God; it is also something we must have daily saving us from sin! This is conversion. My Christian life is not like an elementary classroom. There are no merits and demerits in the Divine eyes of God—at least not on your part or mine. There is simply the blood of Jesus Christ cleansing us from all sin through grace *alone* (1 John 1:7). You see, the adulterous young woman does not leap to her feet and begin a quest of "pleasing" God through her own efforts. No! Instead, her passion burns to live for Him *because* she *is* pleasing to God because of grace!

The point of the story in chapter 2 (taken from John

8) is simple. The focal point is not the absent adulterer. (Scripture says nothing of the man with whom she was caught.) Nor is it the gawking crowd of bystanders. Forget the religious nut-jobs, the accusations, the physical anguish, and the embarrassment. The fact is...she was guilty...and, young friend, so are *you!* I couldn't care less if you have grown up in the church and always heard the accolades of the old ladies as they speak of your generous deeds and likeable demeanor; you are just as guilty before God as that sex-crazed adulteress! Don't pride yourself in your accomplishments. Each one is completely detestable to God...and yes, that includes all those *after* salvation, if done in your own strength. There are no small merit badges in this army. You and I are worthless. We are sinners, plain and simple. We need grace every single day.

And here is the simple truth...yep, you may have guessed it...we *have* grace!

The sin that you commit tomorrow cannot damn you to hell because the penalty has already been paid in full! To this the Pharisees of today shake their head, turning back to a lifestyle of works, not grace. But it remains true nonetheless.

Young person, we must see the One who was for a little while made lower than angels (Heb. 2:9). We must taste of His glory. We MUST understand His grace.

And how better to begin this trek of enlightenment than to first look at the simple, ugly facts—without God, you and I are nothing.

4

A *very* Cool Trade

We have all become like one who is unclean...
Isaiah 64:6

Uniontown, Pennsylvania—Fall 1992

The words had barely escaped Nate's mouth before I gritted my teeth in angry determination. Now you must understand the background of this story to begin comprehending my anger. Nathan—who is my older brother by eighteen months—was my bitter rival growing up. Whether it was wiffle ball in the backyard, a board game in the family room, basketball on the asphalt, or any other contest that young boys could dream up, we would battle one another until we were exhausted, and occasionally bloodied. No doubt God was educating me in the ways of humility all those years, and I received a great education because Nate won nearly every event. Of course, Nate was older, but he was also quite a bit stronger and until

I hit the age of sixteen, he was forever a head taller than I. My blame would be leveled at his height...or age...and he would harass me for the whining child that I was...and thus the battles raged on.

This particular day we were in eastern Pennsylvania. My father—who has been an evangelist for the entirety of my life—was speaking in a church that week. Our 1990 *Holiday Rambler*—which only lived up to the second of those names—was hooked up alongside the church building. Following our duties of connecting the power cords and water lines, we boys began our weekly church exploration, looking for anything to delve into. As it turned out this particular church had nothing for young boys—no ping-pong tables in the basement, no library with dozens of novels, no mowed lawn for catch. So, removing the cords that held my bike to the rack on the front of the motor home, I decided to embark on one of my countless excursions to see the beauty of eastern PA.

I loved my bike. It was nothing super special to anyone else. A *Huffy*, 10-speed, mountain bike, it had come off the sales rack at *Wal-Mart*, but it was my prized possession. At twelve years old I considered myself to be "the next Lance Armstrong" (or early '90s equivalent). I was quite proud of the fact that my bicycle had touched the ground in over one half of the states in the Union and five Canadian provinces. "The most traveled bike in the world!" I often dubbed it...which I realize now was just another of my horrid misconceptions.

However, you can begin to see why I grew so determined that lazy, autumn afternoon. Nate had come up wheeling another bike, which upon Nate's request, the pastor had scrounged up for him. I gazed at his bike and laughed, "What're you doing with *that?*"

He only smiled in response. The bike he toted looked like something straight out of the '60s. It had the banana seat, funky handlebars with individual finger grips, and ridiculously thick tires. Rust covered the frame, the chain clanked noisily, and the ripped seat allowed yellow foam to peek through the faded print. Whenever he squeezed the breaks, the bike would squeal in protest. For a while we just circled the parking lot, laughing at his squeaky mess of a bicycle.

The parking lot began at the vestibule leading into the auditorium of the church. From the glass doors of the vestibule, the asphalt progressed downhill and then to the right, where it circled a concrete island slab stretching the length of the parking area. After circling the island, the lot ran back by the vestibule and out to the main highway. From a young boy's perspective, the lot appeared a perfect raceway, and it is then that the challenge came.

"Hey, Aaron," Nate called, "betcha' I beat ya' in a race around this parking lot!"

"Yea, right," I replied, trying to sound more confident than I felt. "Man, me and my bike would destroy you!"

So within minutes there we stood. We both clutched the handle bars of our bikes...we both pressed one foot against the right hand peddle...we both waited for our sister Hannah to yell, "To your mark . . ." I looked over at Nate as I wiped my nose on the sleeve of my T-shirt and bit my lip. "Get set . . ." My hands unmercifully squeezed the grips. My left leg shook from the bursts of adrenaline. "GO!"

Like a shot we were off! My legs pumped furiously as we flew down the decline. The wind brought tears to my eyes, which flowed unchecked across my face. I rounded the first turn and with a slight lead I felt the excitement shooting through my body. I peddled even faster! Glancing back, I saw Nate right on my heels, madly giving it all he had.

"Come on, Aaron!" I silently cheered. Flying past our parked RV, I came to the first sharp corner. Of course, Nate did the smart thing and slowed down slightly, brakes screaming; I, revealing the stupidity that is, at times, Aaron Currin, did not.

My ten-speed hit a patch of loose gravel, and in horrified anguish, I felt my bike sliding out from underneath me. Everything went into slow motion. My heart cried "no" as I saw my brother whip by! The rough concrete bit into my flesh, peeling the skin away from my left leg and hands. My shoulder crashed into the ground as my bike slid a few feet away.

The scene was a mess. My hands and knees oozed blood. As I sat in pain, dismal at my bitter defeat, Mom and my sisters came running. I remember grimacing as mom later wiped away what dirt she could, wrapping my leg in a white bandage. Nate—the victor—stood in what appeared to be silent concern, but I knew that I would hear about his triumph for days to come.

It was the following afternoon that my bandages were stripped away. The scene of those filthy rags was revolting. Coated across the inside was the dried, yellowish-brown medication mom had applied to my wounds. Accompanying the medicine was a mixture of dehydrated blood and soot. These three components, along with the sweat that had stagnated under those bandages for 24 hours, combined to form a very gut-wrenching odor. Those rags were certainly not an award that I wished to set alongside my glossy plaques and trophies back home. They were disgusting to me...and therefore, the first chance I had, I tossed them in the garbage.

Looking through a Holy Lens

It is a sad reality that many who claim to have experienced salvation don't have a clue what it really means to be redeemed and set free. They say they are Christians, but can't tell you what makes them different from everyone else...except that they're "saved." Far too many teens I meet think of themselves as fairly good people. But the truth is that drugs, alcohol abuse, and premarital sex don't *make* a guy or a girl wicked. The things you do or don't do are just the result of the evil that already saturates your life. Therefore, whenever someone indulges in sin, they are only demonstrating the evil already present in their hearts. Whether you are sexually moral or scathed by STDs, a churchgoer or an atheist, you are a sinner, separate from God and desperately in need of grace (Rom. 3:10).

Sadly, there are many young people who would never state it, but down deep they believe that somehow by going to church each Sunday, playing a guitar for the teen worship band, reading their Bibles, or participating in other "religious" activities, God hails them a "good kid," giving them a wink and a pat on the shoulder. If you fall into this mindset, then you are, in essence, just like the Pharisees in Jesus' day and are therefore treading in extremely dangerous waters.

What you must understand is that the Creator looks upon all righteous deeds, all charitable acts, and sees them as I saw those soiled bandages that had covered my wounds. *We have all become like one who is unclean, and all our righteous deeds are like a polluted garment* (Isaiah 64:6). Fine, we have—as orthodox believers—no problem agreeing with this. Sure, our good works do not merit us favor in the eyes of the holy One *before salvation.* But is that it? For some teens that answer is "yes," and that is where they go wrong. We feel that this verse only applies to our state *prior to* conversion, but...

> **Whether before or after the moment of my salvation, any "good" works that I do in my own strength, trying to please God, are like detestable bandages.**

Yes, my "holy" or praiseworthy acts, and yours, are polluted rags of nothingness! That is why the apostle Paul writes in Philippians 3:8, *For His sake (Christ Jesus my Lord) I have suffered the loss of all things, and count them as rubbish, in order that I main gain Christ!* You see, friend, Paul was not looking through the eyes of depraved men, but he was glancing through the "holy lens" of the Almighty Lord of Heaven. Upon seeing the worthlessness of his "holy manners," he cries out that they are detestable in comparison to the merits of Christ!

The Greek word for rubbish in verse 8 can also be translated "human waste." Pardon the vivid analogy for a moment, but it is essential that we fully grasp this truth.

If you have ever walked into a public restroom and swung open the stall only to find that the person before you had been ill and neglected to flush, you were repulsed I am sure. With that image of sour sewage resting in your mind, you can begin to get a brief, though somewhat grotesque picture of what God sees when His child—whom He has bought freedom for with the life of His Son—brings before Him his or her own waste and smiles proudly, as the sewage drips from soiled hands. Friends, we all must recognize that as we look through the holy lens of a holy God, our works will never bring about His smile. It is absolutely necessary to grasp the truth that our works, which are useless in gaining the favor or God before salvation, *are just as useless in maintaining that favor following salvation!*

Yet we continue to believe that God's response to our good actions will be somehow different than my response to those despicable rags that covered my wounds as a twelve-year-old boy. We suppose that our Father will show that smile because, after all, we tried as hard as we could, and He will take those repulsive rags of dried medication and filth, reeking of blood and sweat, and place them in His trophy case alongside the pure merits of His Son.

Friend, as ridiculous as this sounds, to equate our righteous works with the merits of Christ is exactly what we are claiming when we say or believe that we are earning the smile of God through what we do or don't do as a Christian. Because of the disobedience of Adam in Eden your entire being is polluted by sin. From the moment your life or mine began in the womb, we were creatures of darkness (Ps. 51:5). Since the point of our birth, as we emerged from our mothers, kicking and screaming, we have been liars at heart (Ps. 58:3). And each one of us—despite how clean we appear when compared with the failure of others—are by nature the children of destruction and dead in our trespasses (Eph. 2:1, 3). Our sins were a stench in the nose of God and so detestable in His sight that He could not stand to look upon us. We were racing toward damnation, incapable of even choosing right (Rom. 3:11) because our minds told us that the way we were running *was* the right path (Prov. 14:12), and suddenly God slammed the cross down in our way (Col. 1:20)! By His grace and mercy, *He* called us who are now saved to live in eternal fellowship with Him (Eph. 2:4, 5; 1 John 1:7), and this *He* did through the death of Christ Jesus (Eph. 1:7). Now we are the very sons and daughters of God (John 1:12).

How insane of us then—even borderline blasphemous—to look upon the majesty of Christ and the mercy He demonstrated toward us, and walk away telling ourselves that we must now *do* something to keep His favor! No, friend, we have His pleasure, for some reason that we will never understand

He chose to be crushed so that His Father could find pleasure in us!

And no amount of evil we do...or good for that matter...will ever cause Him to love us more or love us less. No, nothing can or ever will separate us from the unchanging merciful love of God our Father (Rom. 8:38–39).

You see, friend, we were maggots of misery, and now

we are children of mercy! What a mind-blowing trade for us! Everything in exchange for nothing! Amazing grace? I sure think so.

5

living Dead?

A voice on the barren heights is heard, the
weeping and pleading of Israel's sons because
they have perverted their way; they have
forgotten the Lord their God. Jeremiah 3:21

So what's the deal? What is our problem?

Please, don't patronize yourself with big words or profound statements. Don't shift the blame to Hollywood, the White House, liberals, Democrats, Republicans, musicians, denominations, or even your local church. Let's just be honest—you and I. What is wrong with the Christianity of the twenty-first century? Is it boring speakers? Is it hypocrisy? Is it that we praise entertainers and athletes? Is it that we worship the face we spends hours gazing at in the mirror? Is it the absence of genuine love? Why are there so many completely content, passionless teens in youth groups? Why are uncountable multitudes of believers sleeping comfortably in their padded church pews? What is wrong?

The answer is simple. We have forgotten. Forgotten who we were and forgotten Who He is!

We as believers have given way to the god of sex. We have doubled under the weight of our own arrogance. We drown in bitterness, as hatred flows from hearts that profess to know the God of love. Obscenity spews from the lips of teenagers who have grown up in churches. Disrespect is at an all-time high.

The state of many college and teen groups in the church today is frightening. Young people pride themselves on how much of a rebel *against* grace they can be. A worship service consists of trying to impress the guy or girl across the room, instead of finding pleasure in the God Who supposedly lives inside! Thousands of unchanged sinners lift their hands to worship or stare at the speaker over a highlighted Bible having never understood or merely forgotten the reality of the cross. Oh yea, we talk about the cross...we even have mega-blockbuster films depicting the anguish of the cross. But in our every day life we live as if it is only a piece of wood on which a good man died a long time ago. It has no relevance to the life of a college student as he or she just tries to make it to that first-hour class each morning. It does not impact a young athlete vying for that starting quarterback spot. It can't guide the academic whiz shooting for scholastic perfection and the full-ride to an Ivy league university.

You know, every act of wickedness and the overwhelming apathy that sweeps across young people today did not occur instantaneously. Evil and apathy flow simply from hearts that have forgotten...what we were saved from and what grace really accomplished. Forgotten Christ and forgotten the cross.

It all began when we grew busy...or fell in love...or tried to defend our faith through worldly means.

Our focus on Christ dissolved beside the X-Box controller, the football helmet, or the report card.

The Word of God was abandoned and our view of the cross-work of His Son vanished beneath the fog of what the apostles called "worldliness." Therefore, having forgotten the true core of our existence, we are content and happy in our spiritual darkness. We are blinded to the fact that true salvation brings complete forgiveness and adoption into the family of the Creator. We ignore the truth that the cross *is* relevant today.

Of course, any true believer would say no to this claim. Though others might ignore the cross you, no doubt, will readily admit that what happened on Calvary was necessary because without the blood of God's Son we would all still be lost in sin, right?

Young person, while it was crucial that Christ shed His blood for our salvation, we cannot miss the fact that it was also completely necessary that He die for our *sanctification!* That is, His death on Calvary was absolutely essential so that we could have that grace to go on living the Christian life *after* the moment of salvation! As He hung naked and shamed on that Roman cross, He did so not only to save you but also to carry you as a Christian. The simplest truth I can utter to any true believer in Christ is this: Because of the broken body of Jesus Christ, you have forever gained the smile of God the Father! He is now *your* Father. He is forever *your* Friend. Through His sacrifice, we have life and we have complete forgiveness. There remains absolutely no condemnation for us who belong to Him (Rom. 8:1).

If you have chosen to embrace the cross as your forgiveness and freedom, throwing off the robe of sin and accepting the title of God's own child, then you are bathing in a pool of grace! We don't have to fret about trying to make God happy. As we were helplessly flailing toward a place of damnation the Creator God cared enough to sweep down, sacrifice Himself, and catch us before we crashed. *He* is incredible! Not you. *He* is the Savior! Not your "sinner's prayer." *He* is worthy! Not your spiritual accomplishments. Gather all your trophies of Christian victory together...and then watch Christ Jesus toss them into the same pile of dung in which all your sins lie before covering it all with His blood.

That is the primary point of the narrative in John 8. Not that an adulterous woman had sinned—because we all have...the prelude, plot, and conclusion all zone in on that one phrase from the lips of the only Man who never slipped up, stumbled, or sinned: "I don't condemn you either."

Wow! That *should* astonish you! Everything wicked you have ever done has ultimately been a hate crime against Him. You were the spittle that clung to His beard. You were the thorns that wounded His brow. You were the nails that severed His nerves and held Him to a splintered tree. That was you! Yet He says to you today, "I'm not condemning you...my child, *you*, are forgiven and free!"

And as young believers, you and I need to be reminded of this forgiveness. Forgetting the cross is not only dangerous...it is fatal. You might claim to know God but do you look to His cross? Do you rejoice in His resilience? Are you saturated in His Word?

Oh, sure, you shed a tear as you sing about the wonderful cross. Youth will jump around, fists pumping the air as they madly cry, "Jesus Rocks!" We will pack out our teen rooms to get our name in a drawing. And yea...every once in a while we will crack open an old, leather-bound Book, read a few lines and feel good about ourselves. But...

the memory of three 9-inch, tapered spikes; Jerusalem thorns; a Roman cat; a royal robe of mockery; and the unspeakable torment of Divine rejection is forgotten.

Against this backdrop the writer of Hebrews asks this rhetorical question: *How shall we escape if we neglect such a great salvation*(Heb. 2:3)? The obvious answer is, *we will not!* It is interesting that the writer does not use the word "reject" in this passage...but to these Jewish citizens who had heard the prophecies of Old Testament Scripture their entire lives, and now knew those prophecies to be fulfilled in the Person of Jesus, the warning was not to *neglect* truth.

If you say that you know Christ (which is what being a Christian really is!), here is my declaration to you: Do not *forget* this truth! Do not neglect or ignore it. Don't be stupid! You were born again by the Spirit of God, through the work of His love and grace...and you will grow in grace only by that same Divine Spirit (Gal. 3:3). Do not look upon the work of Jesus Christ with an apathetic eye. What He did on Calvary was a miracle. That divine, miraculous gift should tug at your inner being every day. It should draw you into a deeper communion with the God who did everything necessary to win your heart.

My friend...now is the time to remember...

6

"Life's not fair!"

So then it depends not on human will or exertion, but
on God, who has mercy. Romans 9:16

"Life's not fair!"

This is a phrase that I hear with increased regularity in youth circles. Standing before congregations of teens all I must do is begin the phrase—"Life is not . . ."—and immediately everyone in the room will finish the declaration—"...fair!" Is this a true statement? Is life fair? And if we say no—or yes for that matter—by what yardstick are we measuring fairness?

A Bad Break

It was my senior year in high school. My team—the Maranatha Christian Eagles—had coasted through the regular season, annihilating teams with a full-court press defense, blazing three point-shooting, quick interior penetration, and an average of 90 points per game. As one of the captains I was pumped about the season ending tournament. We had taken home the championship the year before, and the team had grown even stronger and more disciplined throughout this season. There would be only one true test in the tournament—a squad that we could encounter only in the semi-finals.

We came out on top by almost 30 points the first game of the tournament with our starting five riding the bench throughout the final period. The next game was that semi-final contest against our rival school—the school that was supposed to be "the test." With adrenaline pounding we blew through the semi-final game, winning by 31 points! Immediately following that game, the celebration began. Sure, the championship wasn't technically for 24 hours, but to us this had been the true challenge. The team we were to face the following afternoon was weak, with poor shooters and lousy ball handlers. We figured we would steam-roll them, flying to our second championship title in as many seasons.

The next day came though, and the Eagles hit a wall. We could not shoot, our passing was horrid, we botched easy lay-ups, and with twenty seconds left in the championship game, we called a time-out trailing by five. I recall sitting on the bench and mopping sweat from my forehead, all the while knowing that I had to do something to keep my team from taking this loss.

The huddle broke. We drove the ball quickly up the court, but to our opponents credit, they stifled us. We could not get off a good shot. Finally, I caught the ball in the corner with just a few seconds remaining. Feet squared behind the three-point arc, I felt the seams of the ball, bent my knees and in one fluid motion—which I had done perfectly a thousand times before—accelerated from the floor. Extending my arms, I let the ball roll off my fingers and flicked my wrist. All eyes watched the orange sphere spiral through the air. The ball descended and I held my breath. Barely grazing the cylinder, the basketball fell short. One of my teammates grabbed the rebound and laid it in the hoop, but seconds later the blaring of the horn announced the verdict. We had lost by three points, 45–42—our lowest scoring total of the season.

Sweats in hand, I stormed into the locker room. Throwing my water bottle I shouted at the top of my lungs the slogan we all love to abuse: "*That is not fair!*"

Now you may have had a tough experience like this game for me. Maybe your boyfriend dumped you, girls; you broke your leg the first game of football season, guys. Perhaps your pain was much worse than either of these scenarios: a parent died or your best friend was diagnosed with cancer. Whatever the situation, perhaps in that moment of grief you too declared that life had treated you unfairly. And honestly, from a human perspective, life is hardly ever viewed as fair.

We could discuss God—the Giver of life—and speak of how we should not complain about circumstances around us because He has given us this life and everything good to enjoy for His glory. However, that is not the particular focus of this book. As I stated, from our outlook, life—in our eyes—is generally unfair. Now however, there is a bigger question that must be brought up and answered:

Is God fair?

Dare I even ask such a question to young believers? To say no to this query defies all that is orthodox to our understanding! Is God fair? The response from thousands of lips would resound—*Yes! He is always fair!*

But is He really? Possibly you are ready too shred this book if I even so much as insinuate that God is unfair, and at one time I would have done the same, but Biblically we must consider the evidence in order to accurately answer this question.

Scripture tells us in Romans 9:13 that God loved Jacob and He hated Esau. This passage is undeniably addressing the doctrine of election. Does it seem fair that God chooses certain people to go to Heaven? Paul answers the arguments before they even have a chance to surface: *What shall we say then? Is there injustice on God's part? By no means!*

"You see, Aaron!" you might cry. "God is always fair for He is never *unjust!*" But that, my friend, is just the problem. Your response to my question above might have been just this: "God is always just!" However, I did not ask you about the justice of the Godhead; I ask about His fairness. The difference between justice and fairness is night and day...

What's up with being fair?

It was late November of my sophomore year in college. I had missed Thanksgiving with my family the previous year, but through determination and persistence I had persuaded my best friend, Sam (whom we all called Dagger), to drive the 1,000-mile trek from northern Wisconsin to Gainesville, Georgia. We left school on Wednesday afternoon and purposed to drive through the night so I could surprise my mom the next morning and eat Thanksgiving dinner with the family.

Dagger grew sleepy around eleven so I took the wheel. After only an hour of driving through the state of Illinois I heard the shrill siren directly behind the royal blue *Pontiac Grand Prix* I was navigating. Coasting to the side of the road, I placed my hands in the classic 10–2 position to await the verdict. Moments later the officer informed me that I had been traveling 82 in a 65 mph zone. I tried pleading my case, giving him all the reasons why I had been speeding and crying about how I had not been home in months. Nevertheless, in spite of my pleas, I had broken the law and I was slapped with a $75 fine.

A Sweet Dose of Mercy

It was July of 2002. The sun was out in full fury, and after completing a few tennis matches and a stint at the pool, my friend, Jonathan, and I decided to grab something to drink. Stopping off at a gas station in route to the restaurant, I filled up the tank, hopped back in the driver's seat, and pulled out of the service station. Hanging a quick U-turn at the light, I coasted into the right lane of traffic. It was then I noticed the blue strobe lights filling my rear-view mirror.

Grimacing, I pulled over on the shoulder and shut the engine. The officer was quick to inform me that I had made an illegal turn and hindered the flow of traffic. In addition to this, I was not wearing my seat belt and not carrying my license—four violations at once! As the officer made his way back to his patrol car, my head throbbed at the thought of how much I would be fined for this offense. However, when the officer returned to stand next to my window he handed me a pink slip informing me that he was only going to give me a warning this time. I was shocked by the news! I couldn't believe it. I remember smiling to Jon as the officer walked away, realizing that I had received extraordinary mercy.

Fairness and Mercy equals Justice?

Now my question is, in which instance was justice served? In the first encounter, I received what I actually deserved. In the second meeting, I didn't. That initial time I was met with fairness. In the second instance, I was given mercy. However, to answer the preceding question...

both times I encountered justice.

How could this be in two diametrically opposed outcomes? The answer rests in the position of authority. Whatever the officer decided was what indeed was the *just* thing because he had been given the place of authority over me in those instances. Both times I deserved a ticket and the fair thing would have been for me to receive it. Therefore, when I received the fine I could not complain. On the other hand, though, when presented with mercy, I was extremely thankful and did not see either police officer as being inconsistent with *justice* in the least.

So now we turn back to our original query: *Is God always fair?* Well, as we saw in the previous chapter, we are all wicked individuals, who are naturally rebels against

His law. God's wrath burns in righteous hatred against sin; consequently the *fair* payment for each sinner is an eternity in hell (Rom. 6:23). We all deserve eternal punishment for our rebellious heart as evidenced by our numerous transgressions. Therefore, if God were always *fair* we would be in the Lake of Fire at this very moment. You see, friend, whenever we receive anything good in our lives—spiritually or monetarily—God is not granting us what we deserve; therefore, He is acting—by definition—in an unfair way.

Whenever an unrepentant person, young or old, dies, they are damned for all of time without end. Never again will they see light. Never again will they feel comfort. Never again will they be offered peace—and reject it. This is fair *and* this is just.

However, when God imparts life to the spiritually dead, draws them to Himself, and they in faith forsake their wickedness, they become children of light, receiving eternal life. This is possible only through the merit of Christ's blood. To think that the righteous Creator chose us to be the special objects of his infinite love is amazing. Yet He did...for His glory...for our good...and in doing this He was not *fair*...but *He was absolutely just once more* (Eph. 1:4).

How could this be? I have to smile, for the mystery is revealed in the holy authority of God. He decides what is right and whatever He decides is ultimately just. We need to be reminded daily that...

**justice is not what we presume it to be;
but it is what God declares it to be!**

He is always just for He alone defines justice. As humans, we cannot totally understand His decrees because He is *not* human.

As stated above, we must never equate what is just with what is fair. We are—owing to our sinful nature—cut off from God and have no right to ever taste of His blessings. It would be perfectly *fair* for the Lord to leave us all in our helpless condition and show love to none of us. And from that blackened picture of death and hell, liberation through the blood of Jesus sparkles like a million crystals with golden magnificence.

Why He loved us we will never know, but the simple, incredible truth remains that though we did not love Him, He chose to love us, and in that love sent Christ to cover our sin through His atonement (1 John 4:10). We can never say enough about the love of Christ our Redeemer; the mercy of Christ our Savior, and the grace of Christ our God!

If Christ had not willingly chosen to be crushed for our sins, then we *all* would have been forever lost. God was not obligated to save us; yet He did. This is the beginning to understanding how to live zealously as a young believer. Is God fair? To many, yes. To those of us who are saved, an adamant *no!* He is always just, but when He knocks us off our feet with His grace and forgives us for every rebellious act *against* Himself, He is not fair. He is extremely rich in mercy (Eph. 2:4).

So can we reply against His decrees? No way. We must never forget that He is GOD! Try to fit Him into logic and you will fail. Let emotions shape your view of Him, and you will fall into error. Always bear in mind that this whole issue we are studying hinges on that one simple phrase...

He is God.

Don't forget it. Don't look past it. Don't seek anything more. Simply remember it.

7

A God Who *breathes*

Christ himself was a Jew as far as His human
nature was concerned. And He is God!
Romans 9:5 NLT

As we have now stated, the cross is the foundation of Christianity. Without the cross, our faith is meaningless. Without the cross, we could never have the grace we see in Chapter Two. Yet we so often overlook the wounded Son; the Lamb of God who was led to the slaughter (Isaiah 53:7). What we need more than anything is a fresh look at Jesus Christ. We need that reminder.

Who was He?

He was a man.

Totally complete in His humanity, Jesus faced all the temptations that you and I encounter on a daily basis

(Heb. 4:15). The beloved disciple John wrote that Jesus actually *became flesh and made his dwelling among us* (John 1:14, NIV).

I have always loved the Christmas holidays. There is—despite the outer cold of most North American climates—an inner warmth in hearts around the world. I recall Christmas Days as just a small boy. My dad had his video recorder; my mom was passing out the gifts; my sisters were shrieking with joyful ecstasy, as Nate and I compared baseball cards. Fresh ginger bread men cooled on the kitchen table while candles reflected a luminous glow throughout our home. Trees, adorned with colorful lights and ornaments of every shape and size...visits to the relatives...hugs and more gifts...caroling on a front porch...and of course, the traditional Christmas story read from the Gospel of Luke.

Despite this reading and the very core of why we as Christians celebrate this holiday...despite our cute clichés of "Jesus is the reason for the season"...and despite our many promoted plays with a class full of kindergarten students portraying Mary, Joseph, and three poorly-dressed wise men, we have lost that Man of deity in the middle of all the hoopla. We wink at the parents as a pretty, little, blonde-haired angel makes a declaration to a group of wide-eyed shepherds and stuffed sheep. Yet we overlook the significance of the angel's radical declaration to those shepherds. *"For unto you is born this day in the city of David a Savior, who is Christ the Lord!"* (Luke 2:11)

Yes, Jesus, the Son of God humbled Himself and was fashioned just like a man (Phil. 2:7). He hungered for food and ate (Matt. 4:2), He grew tired and slept (Mark 4:38),

He cried (John 11:35), and He felt pain (John 19:1–3). These are all characteristics of humanity. God Himself— separate from the flesh He formed—would never hunger, sleep, cry, or agonize physically. Yet He decided to robe Himself in the cloak of true humankind and live for over 30 years upon this earth.

Who is He?

He is God.

Though He *became* a man, He never ceased from being divine. Putting on humanity, He did not put off His deity. From eternity past Jesus Christ has always been the very God of gods (John 8:58). This was declared from the pen of the prophet Isaiah (Isa. 9:6). This was written by the hand of the apostle Paul (Rom. 9:5). This was announced by the beloved disciple (John 1:1). This was proclaimed by God the Father (Heb. 1:8). And this was spoken by the Son Himself (John 10:30).

He is complete in His Divinity. No part of His being as a man was not totally consumed with holiness (Luke 1:35). Though He daily walked among rebels of sin, He never on any occasion committed or even thought anything crafted in wickedness (2 Cor. 5:21). He was spotless (1 Peter 1:19). He absolutely loved righteousness for He is the essence of all that is right (Heb. 1:9).

A Little Science

Now don't frown upon me, friend. I meet very few teens and young adults who enjoy the study of science, and since my third grade year I have been in that majority. As a student, and a poorly disciplined one at that, the most hated course for me throughout high school and college was a science class. I absolutely despised it! Just ask my poor chemistry tutor. I struggled in biology and that crazy periodic table drove me insane. However, there is an amazing truth that can be seen through this subject, though perhaps just one.

Often at college I would get stressed out with projects, relationships, and anything else feasibly imaginable. On these occasions, I would wander out into the soccer field, which was set on the backside of campus. Lying down in the cool grass, I gazed up into the night sky, and with the stars beaming like grand spotlights overhead, my cries to God could frequently be heard.

I have always loved the stars. There is something peaceful about a moonlit night and a blanket of black, spangled with thousands of pinpoints of light. Sitting on a beach at night, listening to the waves wash up on the sandy shore and staring into that vast canopy called space is my idea of genuine relaxation.

On nights at college, as well as any other evenings when I gazed at the stars I was repeatedly reminded of the overwhelming greatness of God. Our planet, the earth, is 25,000 miles around. Yet did you know that if you could somehow take 1 million planets the size of this earth and drop them into the sun, you would still have enough room left over inside the sun for hundreds of thousands more earths. That's pretty incredible.

I love velocity. I confess that I love the adrenaline rush of flying around a corner at a rather reckless speed. But light speed is something that blows my mind and truly astonishes me. In case you didn't know, light travels at 186,000 miles per second! For a moment let us imagine that we could somehow jump on board a space ship, slam the door, crank the engine, and with fire blazing beneath us and a tank full of petroleum, blast away at the speed of light! In the space of a just two seconds we would have shot past the earth's moon wildly traveling at the shocking rate of over 11 million miles every minute! At that incredible speed, it would take us just over two minutes to reach the planet Venus. If we decided to ride in the opposite direction of the sun though, with our destination set on the North Star—which is 400 trillion miles away from our planet—it would take us over 68 *years* to reach our destination! However, the North Star is still well inside the confines of man's knowledge of space. Are you beginning to get the picture?

There are stars thousands of times the size of the sun. There are nine different planets that we can see from earth, each with its own unique design. Yet all of this grand design is direct from the hand of God (Gen. 1:1), and here is the even greater truth, which truly baffles me. This entire magnificently vast universe fits comfortably in that hand. He simply stretches out His fingers, and from His thumb to His pinky He can measure the entirety of the galaxies of all space—not just that which is known to mankind (Isa. 40:12).

To look at the earth on which we live is cause for amazement. To see a flock of geese fly south in the winter having not been *commanded* to do so—that is remarkable. To witness the changing seasons each year, to behold a small acorn transformed into a powerful oak, to see rain fall from white fluffs of nothingness so that the land is fertile and well watered—these, my friend, are incredible marks of Divine genius.

Consider the complexity of your own body. Nothing that mankind has ever created moves with the smoothness of your ball-and-socket joint between your forearm and your upper arm. What about our feet? Did you know without our toes we would have no way of balancing ourselves? Yea, we are strangely intricate—and divinely crafted.

It is pure stupidity that would drive a person to declare that all of this *creation* came about without a grand *Creator.* There is a Creator—a God who has formed time, space, and matter. There exists a supernatural Entity who stretches out His fingers to measure that breathtaking universe; a Deity who shaped the earth, and then constructed mankind (Gen. 1:27). And...

according to Hebrews, Chapter One, that Creator God has a name, the name of Jesus Christ.

Yet despite His perfection and beauty, His Creatorship and Divine brilliance, He delivered Himself up into the hands of lawless men (Acts 2:23). God became Man and sentenced Himself to die the most horrific death mankind in all his vileness could dream up.

8

The Agony of *victory*

Christ has redeemed us…by becoming a curse for us.
Galatians 3:13

Jerusalem, 30 a.d.

For a brief moment in time, you and I have been thrust back through the corridors of history. We find ourselves in the midst of an angry mob of people who are absolutely oblivious to our existence. They all scream, and you cover your ears and turn back to look at me.

Mouthing the words, *"Too loud here . . ."* you wave me to follow you as you begin shoving your way through the masses. Feeling as if we were in a swarming nest of bees, we push and claw our way along. The mob seems focused on one point, and as we shift our eyes to see the object of their focus, we are transfixed. Before us stands a solitary Man. He appears winded and fatigued. Irons on His wrists are biting through His flesh. He is calm though. There sits the high priest, looking smug and confident. Indictments pour out from the lips of accusers against the Man the crowd calls Jesus. We simply gawk in wonder.

Finally, the high priest, whose name we discover is Caiaphas, calls for quite and asks the Man, Jesus, about His teaching. The condemned Man's response is very simple: *"Everything has been said openly...ask those who have heard my message."*

As if divinely connected to Him, we are swept away. We behold Jesus dragged from one bar to another. He is condemned by the Sanhedrin, He is mocked by Herod, and then He is tried by Pilate. Then the order comes for Him to be beaten.

Following closely behind the Roman soldiers, we watch as they tie Jesus' hands together and strip Him naked in the morning sunlight. A master of the whip steps forward...a cat of leather tails trailing his own steps hangs loosely in his hand. The cat holds nine tails. Each tail possesses sharp objects woven into the leather. The point of the cat is not necessarily to beat a man. The only stipulation for a thrashing under Roman law is that the flesh has to be hanging in visible ribbons. Therefore, the purpose of the cat is ultimately mutilation.

As the whip master pulls back his arm and releases the cat, there is no loud snap as a whip makes in a lashing. Instead, all that is heard is the crack of leather against the skin of this Man, Jesus. Each leather strap wraps around the torso, legs, arms, and even the face of the condemned. The sharp stones and blades woven into the tails dig into His flesh. Just as the tails settle the master violently jerks the cat back! The tails, having dug deep into the soft tissue of Jesus, respond to the silent command. As though urging Him to return with them to the whip master, the leather strands of pain uproot his flesh, as the iron shackles on His wrists forbid an escape. The skin on His stomach, back, and face is literally torn into bloody strands of flesh before our gawking eyes. Blood spatters the ground, and the cries of the condemned Man reverberate throughout the Praetorian. Cheers ascend from the spectators. The cat falls again...and again...and again...

Repeatedly the nine tails tear away His flesh until the bloodied stump of what might be a man is all that remains (Isa. 52:28).

His beard—now covered in His own blood—is ripped from His face (Isa. 50:6). In anguish He grits His teeth against the intense agony.

He is reviled, blasphemed, and mocked. The salty spittle of rank men streaks His bared cheekbones. A purple robe of linen is brought forward and draped over the grotesque sinews of exposed muscle and tissue. The oozing blood immediately soaks the fine linen and begins to coagulate. A line of sun hardened thorns, which appear to us more like a column of two inch nails, is twisted and then shoved roughly on His brow digging deeply into His scalp. A soldier takes a rod, and clutching it like a baseball bat He swings with all His strength. The rod strikes the skull of Jesus, propelling the razor-sharp barbs even further into His head and sending the prisoner to the ground. There lies the mass of human flesh shrouded in linen. His breathing consists of short, raspy intakes of air. Pools of blood form under His body.

Lifted to His feet, He is whirled around and His eyes

suddenly flutter open. As if by design, they meet ours. We are frozen. Those eyes are the only thing left telling us that this bloody mass is actually human...and they are locked into our own gaze. Compassion and love are channeled from His heart to ours. Time stands still for both you and me. The truth is dawning upon us slowly; as it will ultimately fall upon that lowly centurion just a few hours from now...*surely this Man is the Son of God!* (Matt. 27:54).

The moment breaks and a Roman soldier heaves the broken body forward. We follow His return to Pilate. The cowardly governor washes his hands, as if clearing his conscience. The sentence falls: "Let Him be crucified!"

Emaciated by continual fasting, He stumbles beneath His heavy cross. Another man is asked to carry the 40 pound beam. Almost crawling and urged on by the sharp point of the spear, Jesus slowly progresses down a road named the Via Delarosa, and up a hill called Golgotha.

Upon reaching the top of the hill, the tragedy now reaches its climax. The linen robe is ripped from his back and the innumerable wounds that were beginning to clot are once again torn open. He is stripped bare before the entire multitude. The bloody furrows on His back flow as one stream of blood. The thorns fastened to His forehead proclaim Him the emperor of all suffering.

Battle-scarred hands roughly seize Him, hurling Him on His back. Splinters dig into tissue that was once wrapped in skin. The transverse wood of the Roman column is beneath Him now. Arms are stretched to their maximum distance; nails are grasped in the hands of the Romans. Hammers fall driving three shafts through the most tender parts of His body. And there...there He lies upon His own place of execution...dying on His cross.

The duty of the murders is not complete though. He must hang upon this cross for the entire world to curse! The beam is lifted to the sky and hovers momentarily above a fissure prepared for the base. Suddenly it drops three feet into place. Indescribable pain shoots throughout His body! The slamming of the beam in its socket has snapped every joint out of place.

The Savior's limbs quiver. His eyes are weighted with tears. He sobs. He is given vinegar to drink. Blasphemies are hurled from the foot of the cross. He bears it all without a word of cruelty. He never raises His voice.

The worst, though, is yet to come. Something we will never completely understand. For all of eternity the Godhead has enjoyed perfect harmony. Never before has the Divine Son been separated to such an extreme from the Father. But now...a weight of severe consequence is draped on the blood soaked shoulder blades of Christ, the Son.

Here it comes. He can feel it. It approaches. It is that cup. The cup that He prayed might pass from Him. He can feel the weight of it. There! We see it! Our transgressions—so black...so revolting—tacked above our prison cells on death row! How miserable we are! Yet...what is this? The Father has reached down through time, as if snatching warrants off the cells of transgressors, He has taken them, in all of their weight and wickedness and is now placing each one in that cup! There is mine...and yours. We see them slide into the cup. Then with crushing weight, He pours out the cup of His wrath—the wrath that we deserve—upon the back of the spotless Son of

God! Instantly the Son—Who has for all of eternity past enjoyed the very presence and fellowship of His Father—senses the terrific burden of sins to be canceled. And then it is that the horrible, foreboding event occurs. The righteous Father slowly turns His back on the Lamb. With a shriek of agony the Son of God cries, *"My God, my God, why hast thou forsaken me?"* (Mark 15:34).

For long hours He hung naked and shamed upon the tree. He was cursed. He was reviled. And as you and I stand by watching this Man suffocate in His own blood, our minds are flooded by one question...just one. *Why? Why has the God who created all that we can see...and touch...and feel...the God of this cosmic universe...the eternal, majestic Lamb...why has He stooped this low?*

And suddenly, with our minds whirling and our hearts overwhelmed we see Him rise for one final breath. The intake of air is sharp and painful. He trembles in agony once more. The cry begins in His chest and bursts forth from those torn and swollen lips. The cry of emancipation! The cry that answers all our questions and tells us the reason why! The cry of a Conquering Savior, sending chills of exaltation up our spines! The cry that shreds the 4-inch thick veil in the temple and leads us into the very holy of holies! The cry of the redeemed.

"It is finished!"

9

A Scream of *Liberation*

Then Jesus shouted out again and He gave
up His spirit. At that moment the curtain in the
temple was torn in two, from top to bottom.
Matthew 27:50–51 NLT

That cry which echoed with such tremendous am-
plification that it rent the veil in the most holy place
completely in two pieces, continues to ripple through the
waters of history and into the 21st century. That cry was
a proclamation that the holy blood of Christ (Acts 20:28)
had done a complete work.

In the first century, criminals were tried and sentenced just as they are today. A judge would write on a
parchment all the crimes of which the criminal was guilty.
The prisoner would then be led away to his cell, the list of
transgressions would be tacked above his door, and there
he would serve out the duration of his sentence. When

the season of punishment expired, the criminal would be brought before the judge once again. The handwritten paper of crimes committed was laid on the table, and the judge would take a stamp and seal the lists of crimes with one word: *Tetelastai*. The word tetelastai simply means, "Paid in full." From that point on, when the ex-con left the prison, if an authority saw him in the streets and attempted to arrest him for previous transgressions, all the criminal had to do was reveal to the officer the stamped word of full payment and his liberty was not in jeopardy.

When Christ went to that cross, hung upon the beams of shame, and cried out that shout of completion his cry was that of "Tetalastai!" The payment had been made, and now for all of eternity we are free!

What does this mean? It simply means that believers are never to observe the law as a means of salvation. Individuals around the world have the mindset—flowing from their fallen nature—that they are pretty good people, not as bad as the next person, and that God, owing to His immeasurable love, will one day weigh their good against their bad and welcome them into Heaven. Many *feel* that there is a law of right and wrong—whether established in their head, human philosophy, or Scripture—and as long as they are "decent human beings" they will be okay in the afterlife. Simply go to a park and as citizens stroll through ask them casually about what will happen to them after they die. It is a guarantee that the overwhelming majority of people will profess that they are going to a better place because of something *they* have done.

Such was the case at the University of Missouri. I traveled there with a pastor and my father when I was eighteen. As we passed out tracts on campus, I was able to talk to student after student. I found that man's opinion of God was extremely humanized and almost every student was relying on his or her merits to gain them eternal life.

Yes, we—as solid believers in the grace of God as revealed by Scripture—would cry foul here. There is a better way to salvation, and we have found it, or should we say, *He* has found us. Sinking in sin He lifted us out by His grace. He made us complete in Him (Col. 2:10).

Where do I find this in the Word? you might ask. The answer rings back from that cry of Christ on the cross: "It is finished!" The debt we owe to God has been canceled... and all sins—past, present, and *future*—have been forever covered by the blood! (Col. 2:13). Therefore...

if I sin tomorrow does God hold that against me? No way!

It is already wiped clean by the redemption of our Savior!

Does this mean He is pleased with my sin? As you have perhaps heard from the lips of a jovial, round-cheeked woman or bellowing minister since you were a small boy or girl, *"God hates the sin and loves the sinner."* Though we will leave the theological accuracy of this statement in reference to all men open for future debate, the incredible truth for you and I as the redeemed community is that this statement is completely accurate.

God always hates acts of wickedness against Him—whether it is an unregenerate man or a child of His family. But His love, favor, and blessing are not based upon deeds. This is where every false religion—including much of so-called Christianity—falls far short of the truth. They base salvation and daily living on things other than Christ Jesus and His grace through the gift of faith (Eph. 2:9).

Are we any different from these false religions and devious cults? Not unless we see the treasure of the cross and how it drastically impacts our lives today. Not unless we begin to understand that our salvation *and* our Christian walk is through the active work of Christ, and our role in the process is actually quite passive. Not unless we once again see God for who He *really* is.

Are you any different?

10

breathing for You

And He did this for you! 1 Peter 1:20b NLT

Each time I meditate on the cross; each time I hear Him scream those words of freedom for my soul; each time I see Him stand, show His wounded hands, and then crush the head of the serpent, I feel tingles creep up my spine. The phenomenal reference, which states that the Son of God will shatter the head of the snake, has such astounding implications for *you and me* (Gen. 3:15).

Yes, we must believe, as Scripture states (Eph.1:7, 12), that Jesus Christ bled for the ultimate glory of God, but a portion of His glory is found in the redemption of sinners. He did this all for *us!* As Galatians 4:4–5 describes: *God sent forth His Son, born of a woman, born under the law, to redeem...*This, my friend, is a marvelous truth. As we journeyed back in time over the previous pages...

endeavoring to grasp just a glimpse of all that the Lamb of God went through we see an intensely personal message.

This life He lived, this death He died, and the blood He poured out on that place of the skull, He actually did for *me!*

STOP HERE!

I know what you are probably saying. Whether you have been in the church your entire life or you are new to the Christian walk—or perhaps are still an unbeliever—you have no doubt heard that Jesus Christ died to save us. So you are saying, "Aaron, when are we gonna' get to the good stuff?"

I have one word to shout for the answer—STOP! Young friend, we are here! This is the "good" stuff! This is what we need. *Christ!* He is it. He is the Christian life. He is our source for daily strength. It is in Him, we find rest! Can't you see it? He died to buy you back from the penalty of your sin! But that's not it! He also died so that you could be free to live with intense passion and unending joy! He suffered so that you could rebel against the status quo of lifeless religion and godless living!

Does this not cause your heart to burn with concentrated passion to see the God of righteousness, Creator of all, whom you have repeatedly offended, suffering there for *you?* Bleeding out His life's breath for *you?* Lifting up His wounded, thorn-studded head, and crying that one holy cry for *you?* My friend, if you are a member of this Divine family...a family not man-made, but established through this holy blood (John 1:13)...then *you* have been bathed in grace. *You* have been washed clean. *You* have been reconciled to God (Heb. 2:10). He sees you not as a sinner, but as a son or daughter. *You* are perfect in the eyes of God! When the Father looks upon you, He sees the righteousness of Jesus Christ.

This, my friend, is not because of anything you have done; it is because of that body, the precious body of a Redeeming God—who did *everything* for *you!* Through His death on that splintered column in the burning heat of the Jerusalem sun, I have forever been dressed in a robe of righteousness. Righteousness, once again, not found in my works (before, or following my salvation), but *the righteousness of God Himself, found through faith in Jesus Christ* (Rom. 3:22).

It was necessary that we took these few chapters to remind ourselves of forgiveness, mercy and grace. We had to look once more, for the hundredth time upon that suffocating, stump, of unrecognizable flesh. We had to learn again about the beauty of His righteousness. Why? Because we as young believers will never burn with a radical passion for God, until we clearly see His radical passion for us! Not only must we see it, we must *taste* it!

Young Christian, your life should be driven by the simplicity that though you deserved hell, you received mercy. Each day you should fall on your knees and with head lifted to Heaven, cry,

"Thank you, God, that through Christ's broken body you have chosen not to be fair!"

11

the source

Grace and truth came through Jesus Christ.
John 1:17

The receiver lay still on the tile floor of my second level, dormitory bathroom. Knees to my chin, I stared at the ceiling from my crouched position between the sink and the shower. It didn't matter that I was resting on a damp bathmat that happened to be soaking through my gym shorts. It didn't matter that my eyes burned from lack of sleep, or that it was now well past two in the morning and I had a first period class in just a few hours. What mattered was the conversation that had just ended.

Attempting to show someone the forgiveness of God over twelve hundred miles of telephone line is extremely difficult. Not accurately understanding it yourself makes matters worse. As I sat, hands on my head, beginning to feel the affects of the soaked floor mat, I realized that I had no clue what transforming grace really meant...and the long phone talk I had suffered through only proved it.

He was a friend...my best friend. He had grown up in a devout, Christian home, and had professed to know Christ from an early age. We had shared common interests throughout adolescence and were extremely close in high school and college, though we attended different schools. Although I knew him well, it was not until the second semester of my junior year in college that I became aware of the full extent of what my friend was involved in. He was an alcoholic, suffering from severe bouts of depression and bi-polar disorder. He smoked marijuana frequently and ultimately tapped into various narcotics to ease his troubled mind. His life was a wreck. Disillusioned with church and Christianity he swore off God, wanting nothing to do with the truth of the Bible.

It was in this state of spiritual darkness that he called me that evening. It was definitely not the first time that he had called me for direction and guidance, but this evening we talked much longer than usual. Life was not a thing he valued any longer. There was no point in going on, he claimed.

I tried to convince him of truth...to show him the grace of God. And it was while I was in the midst of attempting to explain truth that I was slammed with this stark and frightening realization—*I don't even know what grace is!*

Oh, I, too, had grown up in church. I, too, had heard the message of "God's grace" my entire life. I had even preached it, but it finally struck me that night in my dorm room that I—and most of the people I knew—did not understand what Jesus Christ had actively done *to* us on the cross of Calvary. It was that night that I said "no" to a performance mode of Christianity and began to understand Christ and His mercy in a whole new way.

One Set of Footprints

I recall reading the famous story of the *Footprints in the Sand* as a young boy. It hung on the paneled walls of my grandmother's living room. The words were set on a picture of the seashore and surrounded by a gold frame. I thought it was a cool story when I was younger, but as I grew older and began to understand God's grace, I realized that the poem was not actually accurate.

If you recall, the story is about a man who has a dream that he is walking along the beach with the Lord. He sees two sets of footprints in the sand at many points, but only one at some very rough times in his life. He asked the Lord why at those rough moments he had to walk alone without God's strength, to which Christ replied, "In those rough times, it was actually I who was carrying you." The portrayal here is that in our lives God walks beside us and in the moments of greatest weakness or hardship the grace of Christ carries us through.

Though this story brings emotional warmth to many people, the dream is misleading. What it fails to communicate is that the love of the Savior *always* carries us (Ps. 37:23–24). There is never a time in our lives as believers that the Son of God is not holding us up by His grace. *Never are there two sets of footprints in the sand!*

Through the rough trials and the times of peace there is always just that one set of Divine footprints.

When a parent dies in a tragic accident or on our wedding day in the midst of extreme bliss, the mercy of the Redeemer is sustaining us (Ps. 63:8). This is a glimpse of that sustaining grace. This is what believers have through our Source.

The Offer

Today the primary demand of the righteous Father is not to live lives of strict adherence to a set of rules. The charge is not to worship with uncontrollable enthusiasm. Nor is it His decree that we even know Theology (the study of God) to our fullest mental capacity. Rather, the one command that we cannot ignore is that we must take His *Son!* Whoever refuses the Son loses all, but whoever accepts Him inherits all the blessings of God (John 3:36; Eph. 1:3). In the Son we have forgiveness of all wrong. The blood of Jesus now demolishes the sin that was so monstrous in your life and mine.

This, my friend, is the beauty of grace. Christ Jesus—the eternal Son—gave His life so we could bask in the sunlight of His mercy daily so we could drink continually of the grace pouring down on us. And if you have accepted Christ you have *all!*

To us who have been saved He is our all. He is our reconciliation to the Father (Heb. 9:12), our Protector (John 6:28), our Love (Isa. 40:11), our forgiveness (Col. 3:13), and our lives (Col. 3:4).

After that night of misery on the bathroom tiles of

my dorm room, I set out with a mission to uncover biblical grace. I am still growing in my pilgrimage of grace, as are we all, but what I have found to be true is eternally simple: grace is Jesus Christ.

12

When Wearing the Right Thing *really* matters

For our sake he made him to be sin who knew no sin, so
that in him we might become the righteousness of God.

2 Corinthians 5:21

Merry

Nervously, she eyes the dress. Her slender fingers
toy with the embroidery. She cherishes the dress, prides
herself in its beauty. She assumes that others are gazing
upon her and revels in the thought that they desire her
gown for their own. Elegantly she sweeps the gown
around her ankles, pretending to be oblivious to the eyes
she is sure are watching.

Adorning her dress are traits that many of the
other gowns do not possess. Her neckline is festooned
with expensive white lace. Her sleeves are pleated, with
large white puffs ballooning from her shoulders out to

her elbows. The veil is beautiful as well. She has deplet-
ed countless hours on her appearance, lavishing costly
make-up on her features. Ornaments flash from her ears
and sparkle from her neck.

Indeed, much personal preparation has gone into this
day for the young bride, for this is the day she has lived
for her entire life. Within the hour, she will stand before
her groom. She will gaze into his eyes. She will feel his
heart beat for hers. She longs to reach out and touch
him, to be near him. She can picture his face in her mind.
She *knows* it will be the perfect love, for look at her—
she shines with radiance unmatched by any other bride
before or any likely to follow.

With a flourish of sparkling white beauty she smiles,
her teeth even and straight. Her powdered nose crinkles
cutely as she beams, and her eyes flicker with a light
of enthusiastic excitement. It will only be a matter of
moments now.

"Uh, ma'am?" She flinches at the voice behind her.

She has a hard time keeping her eyes fixed to the
mirror, as she looks up to acknowledge the presence at
her back. With an air of annoyance she half-turns, momentarily removing her gaze from the silver glass before
her.

"Yes," came the brusque reply.

"Umm, ma'am, I have been sent with a message." The
voice is that of a man's. It carries with it a rich, baritone
quality, and the hesitation is not one of uneasiness, but
rather a stall to gain her full attention. It does not merit
the desired response.

"I'm listening."

"Well, I kindly ask for your utmost attention, ma'am. What I have to say is of extreme importance."

Heaving a weighty sigh, the soon-to-be bride whirls on her heel to stare the newcomer in the face. He is a jovial looking man. His eyes are bright; his smile ready. He nods at the young woman as if introducing himself. "As I said, I have a message for you."

"Get to it then!" the woman brashly interjects.

"Of course," the newcomer proceeded, "I am the dressmaker, and your name is...?"

"Merry."

"Very good then, Merry. My reason for being here has been appointed by the father of the groom. I am to offer you a new gown."

The young woman scoffs at the man. "You insult me, sir! Your offer is not only undesired, but offensive. I have spent much time and effort on my gown. Look at the fine craftsmanship. Look at the lace. Here, see this remarkable quality!"

The response from the lips of the dressmaker is simple and sober: "Your gown, young Merry, is not good enough."

"What?" cries the bride. "How dare you, sir!"

"I only say this because I know what the groom demands, and your gown is not good enough, ma'am."

Merry's eyes blaze and her face flushes with furious heat. "I know that my groom will love me, for I have done my very best on this dress. It matters not what you say. I do not consider your statements to be true. You are a very cruel man! Why do you presume that your gowns are any fairer than the one I wear?"

"Ma'am, please, understand me," the dressmaker

pleaded. "I care not if you like my gowns, and I realize that it is difficult for you to give up your labors for the merits of another, but this is not *my* desire, Ms. Merry. I am simply called the dressmaker, but the gowns are actually crafted by the groom himself. He has sacrificed more than you can ever imagine to have you arrayed in His garment. For you to wear his gown is what the father of the groom has commanded!"

"You only seek a profit!" bemoaned the young woman.

"Not so, Merry. My dress if free of charge, for it is actually a gift of the father, as I have said. I am just offering it to you. Without it, the groom will never accept you."

"Liar!" she cries. "The groom and his father will love me! They will accept me!" She is at the point of tears, but at the same time she feels an intense anger boiling within. "I know they will!" she concludes. "Now get out of my sight!"

Appearing as though he desires to say more, the dressmaker raises a hand, but the furious bride-to-be whirls back to her mirror. Slowly turning, the man regretfully makes his way to yet another soon-to-be bride.

Give your dresses to others, Merry muses sizing up the other brides. *They may have need of them, but I surely do not.* She once again gazes admirably upon her craftsmanship. *He will accept me; he must. How could he not?* And with this thought in mind, she once again turns to gaze into the mirror.

Mercy

Across the great room another young woman stands

by herself. She, too, has been admiring her own gown. She, too, anxiously waits to hear her name called. She will then step through those doors and come face-to-face with her groom. She is admittedly somewhat nervous. Her dress is beautifully stunning in her eyes, but what if her bridegroom does not think so? This thought has tormented her mind. Surely, he must like her gown, for it is her own creation.

Restlessly rubbing her hands together, she had long ago turned from her own mirror, and with some curiosity now watches the other brides. A certain man piques her interest. The man is short of stature, but confident as he progresses from one bride to another. She wonders what he is speaking of, and hurls speculations around in her mind. As she ponders his message, the man suddenly turns and strides purposefully toward *her.*

Self-consciously she smoothes out her own gown and awaits his arrival.

He smiles broadly, stepping into her presence. "How are you, ma'am?"

"I am well, sir. And you?"

"Quite well," he replies. "Please allow me to introduce myself. My name is the dressmaker." He tilts his head to one side, as his smile widens, "And what might yours be?"

"I am Mercy," replies the girl.

"Well, Mercy, I have something very important to tell you. It concerns your wedding gown."

The girl clutches both sides of the smooth fabric. "What is wrong with it?" Her tone is defensive and the dressmaker spots a look of despair wash over her features.

"I understand that you believe your dress to be beautiful, and to me it appears quite lovely as well. I know you have taken great personal care to keep it looking beautiful, but ma'am, I know the bridegroom personally. He is a close friend, and your gown—I'm afraid—is, very simply, not good enough to merit His love."

"What?" cries Mercy. "Not good enough?" She gazes at him with some skepticism. "Why should I believe you? How am I to be sure that you know my groom?"

"You cannot be sure, but I do, ma'am. His friendship is the greatest I know. Indeed, he is a friend like no other."

"If He is kind as you say, then surely he will accept me as I am."

The dressmaker shakes his head. "Not so, Mercy. If you are clothed in your own gown—despite all the effort you may have put into it—it will not be good enough to unite you to the groom. He *will not* have you."

Tears begin to spill over the lashes of the young woman, but the dressmaker stands undaunted at this show of emotion. "Well, if he will not have me as I am, then he does not deserve me!" wails Mercy.

The dressmaker smiles sympathetically. "Ma'am, I know that is how you see things, but I must be honest. It is you who does not deserve the groom." Her eyes widen in shock, but he continues. "You see, Mercy, he is so good and so kind. Everything that is pure and right is found in the groom. And if you will not wear *his* gown, then you will never be *his* bride."

With her bottom lip protruding and tears streaking her made-up face the young bride shakes her head and turns away from the dressmaker. "Please, leave, sir," she mutters forlornly.

Quietly, slowly, the dressmaker once again turns and shuffles away.

The young woman—anguish and apprehension filling her heart—sinks to a seat in the corner, her back to her own mirror. She hides her face in her hands, sobbing quietly. Perhaps the dressmaker is right. Perhaps she does need a new gown. But—no, no! Her gown is quite good—exceptional. What is wrong with it? Nothing, nothing at all. What...what if what the dressmaker had said is true? What if the groom would not accept her? But...

Her tears had begun to subside when she suddenly becomes conscience of another presence beside her. Head shooting up, her eyes fix upon a solemn, yet caring countenance. The man—another man—has sat down next to her. His dark eyes are penetrating and thoughtful. His demeanor is serene. He is calm. In fact, his very presence brings a sense of tranquility to the young woman.

As he speaks, his voice is soothing to match his demeanor. He does not comfort her with his words, but neither does he condemn her. "You have a decision to make, Mercy." How he knows her name is beyond to her. It is his statement that dominates her attention. The words convince her that a change *is* required, and owing to the fact that she does not know when the doors will open and her name called, it is necessary for her to make the resolution now.

The newcomer continues his discourse. "I have witnessed many drawn conclusions concerning this very thing, and though they made them with steadfast determination, their choices were the wrong decisions. They walked into their appointed ceremonies, young Mercy, wearing their own gowns, and they were rejected by the groom.

"Each time they supposed that they would be the exception—that he would somehow accept them and their imperfect gowns. Each time they compared their flawed garments with the stains of another's. Yet each time, they were turned away from unity with him."

The expressions "imperfect" and "flawed" do not warrant an angry response from the girl, but rather cause her eyes to open to the true blemishes in her own dress. She can now see dark stains marring the front of her clothing. The edges are not smooth as she had imagined and afore saw, instead they are tattered shreds of worn satin ruin. The bodice is deeply soiled and the flowing tresses are slit and frayed. What a pitiful wreck of a wedding gown, and just *now* she sees it. It is as if this man by her side has suddenly opened her eyes.

The voice of the newcomer comes to her again. "Yes, Mercy, it is awful. Though all presume that their wedding clothes are grand—for indeed, all here have made their own gowns too—every garment is just as yours—soiled, tattered, and repulsive. There is no way the groom will accept any dressed as they are."

The young bride lifts her eyes and is suddenly horrified at the sight before her. Young women draped in shredded rags dance before mirrors staring at their own images as if by some miracle they are graced by a beautiful garment of silk. And yet, she herself had been this same way. Only moments ago, she had scoffed the offer of a new dress, but now she desires it more than all else. She cannot bear the thought of being rejected by her groom!

Shifting her eyes to look directly at the man by her side, she asks pointedly, "Who are you, sir?"

A slight smile turns up the corner of his lips: "My name is the Persuader. I am the closest relative of your groom and his father."

"The groom...the groom...he is kind, as some say?"

Another, wider smile. "Very kind. There are none better."

"Then," she stares down at her wretched outfit, "what am I to do about my gown? If he will not have me as I am clothed, then how am I to dress?"

The gentle, comforting Persuader places his hand tenderly on her knee and smiles a smile of triumph. "Have no fear, my dear, sweet Mercy.

There has been a gown prepared expressly for you by the groom ..."

It was as he was saying these words that the young woman saw the dressmaker approaching her again. Overflowing with gratitude that he had not given up on her, Mercy leaps to her feet in joyful exaltation! Before he can speak, she cries aloud, "Oh please, sir...do you have a new gown for me? How I long for a new gown for I have seen my own miserable dress as it is and have been kindly convinced by my good friend here to put off my old garment for that of my groom's!"

The dressmaker beams. "This is the greatest decision you could have made, young Mercy." He moves to stand directly before her, as he continues with the thought, "Now when you stand before your groom he will indeed accept you as his true bride!"

Mercy, overcome with emotion, allows the tears to race unchecked across her cheeks. At her simple request for a new gown, an amazing sense of revitalization washes over her. Her heart is full of joy and no doubts remain. She feels like racing throughout the room and shouting out her newfound beauty for all the other brides to hear. Oh, her previous state had been so dismal. How could she have ever found splendor in *this gown*—this gown of *her own* making?

Her thoughts abruptly cease. Here eyes are transfixed on the gown suddenly clothing her body. It is a beauty unlike anything she had ever seen. She had not changed out of her old dress, but it has nonetheless gone, and in its place hangs this...this majestic...this brilliant...this exquisite beauty. The gown is completely pure. It is without any spot or blemish. She would never have been able to understand this had she not been brought to a point of complete comprehension by her Persuader. She turns now—her new gown radiating absolute purity—to gaze to where her comforter had been seated. He was still there; he would always be there, and his presence is a calm reassurance to the young woman.

She smiles the smile of triumph now for she is clothed in the garment of her groom.

Too Late to Change

Back on the other side of the large room, Merry has finally grown somewhat tired at gazing upon her own beauty, and for a short time decides to sit and watch the other young women. They all hold no comparison to her own magnificence, she vainly muses. Her gown is far more beautiful than any other. Yet all the other women seem happy and content.

Merry has forgotten the harsh words of the dressmaker, but swiftly those words return when she observes him moving throughout the room once again. He stops before another young woman and begins to chat with her. *Ugh!* The very sight of the man repulses young Merry now. She turns away to gaze back into the mirror. How could he not see that this was resplendent?

"Merry!" The name reverberates throughout the room and young Merry's head whirls around. Two identical heralds are standing by the enormous double doors leading out of the room and into the ceremonial auditorium. This is her time!

With graceful speed she makes her way to the doorway, her train trailing behind her. The heralds say nothing as she steps through the entrance and into the grand auditorium. Crowds of witnesses line the walls and fill the center of the great hall. Merry smiles and nods as she passes each one, assuming that they, too, are marveling in the brilliance of the gown she wears. At the front of the auditorium, the center aisle expands, opening into a large expanse into which only two individuals stand—the Groom and His Father.

Presuming that the eyes of the Groom would be full of love had been a false assumption. From his expression, it is apparent that he possesses no love for this woman. He gazes upon her with great contempt and now, for the first time, the young woman begins to believe what the dressmaker had told her to be true.

The voice that rings out comes bearing authority. "Why are you not dressed in the gown of my Son?"

Merry's eyes dart to the man on the left hand side of the groom. He appears elegant and stately. His wisdom shines through his eyes, but now those same eyes rage with an intense fury. The query falls from his lips once again, "Why are you not wearing the gown of my Son?"

Merry swallows hard. "Because I did not...did not believe the dressmaker."

"And why not?"

"Because," she muttered, "I thought my dress was... was good enough." She looks down at her gown and a shriek of horror blasts from deep within her soul. It is no longer beautiful—in fact, it never had been. She had been blinded to the hideous imperfections. Now she sees the gown for what it is—a deplorable heap of utter waste. Every inch of it is covered in filth. The train is tattered. In fact, it barely resembles a wedding dress at all. It is, instead, a soiled garment with no redeemable qualities. Merry's eyes fill with tears once more, but these are not tears of anger.

"You presumed falsely," the father declares. "You are still clothed in your own gown."

"Please, please," the young woman mumbles, falling to her knees. "I beg you; I must have a new one, sir. Please, give me a new gown." She sees no light of hope resonating from the father or the groom. "Please, "she cries aloud, "I need your gown!"

The groom does not appear defeated, but he is some-what saddened by what must occur. Lifting his eyes to look upon the girl he finally remarks, "You have disobeyed my commands. You are not clothed in my garments."

Merry started to say something, but the groom held up his gloved hand.

He did not apologize for what he did now. He simply did it. "Leave."

"Give me another chance!" she weeps.

"You have had your chance; you will *not* receive another." The final proclamation extracted a desperate screech, reaching down into the very soul of the reject-ed bride. The groom stood stoically before her, his arm stretched out and pointing to a dark exit to the left of his father.

"No, no, no!" plead Merry, but the ushers came and lifted her from her kneeling position. "Please!" she screams. They did not hesitate though. The groom had spoken; he must be obeyed.

Dressed in her own gown, and shrieking cries of pro-testation, the young woman was cast out of the ceremo-nial auditorium. As soon as her presence disappeared, her cries vanished as well. The testimony from the lips of the dressmaker had stood true: *dressed in her own rags she could never be the bride of the Son.*

A Nod of Approval

Young Mercy still sits out in the large dressing room. She cannot get over the splendor of the bridegroom's gown. It fits her beautifully. This much was certain; the gown she wore had been fashioned specifically for her. It was not a "one size fits all." This simple truth causes her smile to widen and her heart to warm. *The groom loves me—me.* The personal thought is something she desires to rest upon eternally. His love had sent not only the dress-maker to her, but had also created a gown precisely for her, and accompanying that gown came the Persuader who showed her the errors in her own garment and the beautiful quality of the groom's.

Even now the Persuader sits by her side. He speaks frequently, telling her of the majestic kindness of her groom and assuring her that she will indeed be united to him for he would never reject what he had sacrificed to create. It bothered Mercy none at all that her own beauty and efforts did not merit the love of her groom. She is simply thankful that she had discovered the truth in time.

With a tinge of sadness she observes the dressmaker go from one bride to another, offering each one a beautiful gown, which the groom himself had completed. Each time, these young women, clothed in filth, would gaze upon their rags—as if delighting in them—and then would shake their heads at the proposal.

How foolish they are! thinks Mercy. Yet she fully recognized that had the Persuader not come to her, she never would have accepted the new dress, which now clothed her body. Something that did cause the young woman to smile was the presence of the Persuader. He never left her side, and his company was a great comfort to her.

Deep in thought and reverie, she suddenly hears her name called.

"Mercy!"

She quietly stands and the Persuader stands with her. Two indistinguishable heralds stand on both sides of the mammoth doors leading into the ceremonial hall. She takes a deep breath and smiles. She feels the Persuader take her hand, leading her through the entryway. Turning once more to look at the dressmaker her smile broadens.

He simply waves and then clutches his fist in triumphant praise.

The Persuader continues to lead her, and she is very grateful for his reassurance. As soon as Mercy steps through the doorway lights flood her being. There is a great, innumerable gathering of people. They crowd the auditorium. Those near her gasp at the exquisite feature of the stunning gown she wears. It is indeed flawless and perfect. Compared to the purity of it, all else *is* detestable.

The auditorium into which Mercy steps is magnificent. Hundreds of crystal chandeliers dangle above the multitudes. Each chandelier holds dozens of candles. The auditorium glows with resilient splendor. Everything about the room is superlative, and the young woman's heels make soft imprints in the lush crimson carpet of the center aisle. Yet despite all the beauty surrounding her, Mercy has eyes only for her groom. She has only ever dreamed of what he would be like; it was now for the first time that she is able to see him face to face. And he...

he has eyes only for her.

As she makes her way down the aisle—the Persuader by her side—the groom begins to stride toward her. The two draw closer, until neither can take the momentary separation any longer. Extending his legs, the young groom breaks into a dash toward his bride. Mercy lifts the train of her dress and races to meet her bridegroom. It is in the center of the huge auditorium that the two meet, throwing arms of love around one another. The masses erupt in a thunderous ovation.

With arms rapped around the neck of her groom and crystal tears streaking her face, young Mercy gazes to the front of the room where the father of the groom stands. His face beams and he nods his approval. Words could never express her gratitude to the Persuader. Yes, the Son had indeed personally created her gown, but had it not been for the urging of the Persuader, she never would have seen her need for a new dress. And now she realizes more than ever that she never could have experienced the loving bliss of this moment apart from that gown. She buried her face in the chest of the groom, content to forever rest in the mighty arms of her love.

13

The Nod of *approval*

We are made holy by the sacrifice of the
body of Jesus Christ once for all time.
Hebrews 10:10, Author's Translation

The truth of this amazing account is overwhelming! Each of us, young and old, have an appointment, just as these brides did (Heb. 9:27). We don't know when our name will be called, but when it is we must go—ready or not. Despite the fact that our merits seem pleasant and appealing to us—as they did to the foolish bride, Merry—they are, as we have seen, worthless and detestable before the true Father and His Son (Isa. 64:6).

The dressmaker shows us the messenger of truth (Rom. 10:15). God has set up many here on earth to declare his truth, and though they do this faithfully, often men, women, and young people reject the offer of salvation, choosing to remain wrapped in their own rags of ruin, rather than accept the righteous cloak of the Redeemer. In this state, they will eventually stand before God, and dressed up in wickedness, the blame will fall squarely upon their very own hearts for the dismal attire they wear (John 3:18). The triumphant Son will not be frustrated or disappointed on that Day of Judgment, but with majestic glory He will point to His left and declare to those standing in their own righteousness, "Depart from me into the eternal fires of hell!" (Matt. 7:23). There will be no second chances given. For those who rejected Jesus Christ and His righteousness, an eternity of torment apart from his grace will be their reward (Matt. 25:46).

Young friend, I realize that this is a book; it is not the same as sitting under the preaching of Scripture. But in this moment I want you to see this as a sermon on paper, instead of just a paperback. I sincerely care about you, and the God whom we have discussed for these past several chapters does as well. Why waste time? For many reading these pages, the truth of grace is amazing because it has captured them. However, for some it doesn't mean that much, and that might be due to the fact that they have never experienced this grace of which I write.

Perhaps that is you. You have played the game. Maybe grown up in the church. But the cross and grace and all of Christianity seems pretty empty and abstract to you. Friend, I tell you now what I must for your own good: If you have never made the choice to be a radical follower of Christ, then you do *not* have the smile of God upon you. You are still a rebel of unrighteousness and that eternity of Divine torture is all that awaits you. Please do not comfort yourself with grace if you are like Merry and have never tasted it. I beg you to fall upon His salvation, leave your sin, and find mercy that purifies the soul.

Cast off your garment of wickedness for the robe of righteousness.

For those of us who believe on Christ—trusting in His merits on that Roman column of agony—we will find that a gown of complete righteousness was fashioned for us long ago by the hand of God Himself (Eph. 1:4). Our sins are laid upon the Savior, and His unmerited holiness is mercifully bestowed upon us. Indeed, we are the "bride of Christ" (Rev. 21:9).

This is partly the reason for the names of the two young women in the story. Merry shows us those who attempt to earn salvation through holy living or charitable deeds; Mercy is obviously those who simply cast themselves upon the grace of God through the death of Christ. This is the dynamic message of 2 Corinthians 5:21.

Therefore, because of Him and Him alone, one day when we hear our name called and we step into that grand judgment hall, there will be no condemnation for those of us who are robed in the righteousness of Christ. The Son will wrap His arms of love around us—His true bride—touch our faces with those nail-scarred hands, and will declare: "Well done."

Well done? What have we done? It was His gift to us right? (Eph. 2:9). It was He who laid down His life so we could be dressed in purity correct? (Heb. 10:22). Was it not Christ who sacrificed to clear our record of debt we owed to Him? (1 John 4:10). And was it not the Son who died that horrible death of chapter eight enduring the mockery, the blasphemy, the physical agony, and the Father's rejection?

And He did this so that His Father could look into our eyes and with a smile proclaim, "Welcome home...well done!"

This is what that cross secured for us. This is why He had to go through all He did. To dress us in holiness so we could hear, "Well done!"

Friend, if you have been saved, you are currently and for all of time dressed in the righteous gown of Jesus Christ. Don't become burdened with trying to gain His approval. He is a mighty God, and those He saves He sustains. He will never let you fall. He will hold onto you. And when you stumble in sin, He will pick you up and make you stronger by His grace.

Live in this reality. Rejoice in this grace. Rebel against philosophies that promote religions of merit and disgrace the purity of grace. Look daily to the cross because from those two columns comes the very strength, peace, and passion for us to live victoriously in God. And then, one day, as we enter the courtroom of Heaven, race toward our Savior, and feel His arms wrap around us, we will peer over our Redeemer's shoulder, and—like Mercy—will see the Father Himself nod His approval.

14

God Will

For you were killed, and Your blood
has ransomed people for God.
Revelation 5:9 NLT

I have attended more church services than I can count. My father, as stated previously, was a traveling preacher, so night after night I sat in unfamiliar pews. Throughout high school and into college, I frequented youth rallies and countless worship services. Now I travel with my own ministry. And wherever I go, no matter the denomination or age group, I hear this single phrase that I completely detest: "Let God."

This statement, though often used, borders on the brink of absolute blasphemy. I sincerely despise it! For me, as a finite, lump of clay, to look at you and tell you— as another mere pile of dust—to allow the all-powerful Creator God to do something for you, takes the power out of the hands of God and places it squarely in the lap of a man or woman who still struggles with the way that seems right (Rom. 7). It implies that my decision and resolve holds more authority than the sovereign will of Christ Himself. This statement blatantly humanizes the One who looks upon mankind as grasshoppers (Isa. 40:22)!

We have screwed up in believing that God actually *needs* us at all. We have slipped by convincing ourselves that we have to *let God* do something, which insinuates that He was incapable of doing so without our permission.

What I declare to you now, friend, is not to let God do anything, but rather to behold the God who *has done* everything! His death on Golgotha's column of cruelty was not a *passive* response to a serious predicament. His agony, dear reader, was in the place of sinners, and He actually, *actively* has set men free! Paul writes in Romans 3:24–25 that *now God in His gracious kindness declares us not guilty* (or justified)! *He has done this through Jesus Christ, who has freed us by taking away our sins. For God sent Jesus to take the punishment for our sins...*(NLT). You see, everything about this passage presents an active Savior. He *declares* us not guilty, He *has done* this, He has *freed* us, He has *taken away* sin, He *sent* Christ, but "we *believe*" you declare! Yes, friend, but even our faith is a divine gift that would have been impossible to enact had not God given it to us by His grace (Eph. 2:9).

In writing to the churches in Galatia, Paul states once more that Christ gave Himself for our sins to actively deliver us! (1:4), and again in chapter 4, verse 5 He died to *redeem,* not to make a redemption passively possible for a spiritually lifeless man to take. Jesus Christ, the Lamb of

God, *took* the sin of the world (John 1:29); He *reconciled* us to Himself (2 Cor. 5:18); His blood *brought us near* to the Father (Eph. 2:13); His death *secured* for us an eternal redemption (Heb. 9:12).

I challenge you to go through the New Testament and look at the passages dealing with genuine salvation and reconciliation to God. You will discover that our warped, human mindset has given ourselves too much credit for a work that was accomplished on Calvary in the first century a.d. The reason you or I am saved today is not because we sought for it or believed; we are saved primarily because God chose to die. The basis for living life as a child of God tomorrow is not because of our works, but because God *chose to die.* And the reason why all who have been united to Christ will one day inherit the riches of that celestial city is not because you somehow impressed God or I kept myself in His favor, but—you guessed it—it is because God chose to die, *for you!*

Let this sink in. See the truth drowning out the lies. Watch the blood fall upon you in that tidal wave of grace. Bask in His death *for you.* Dance in His grace poured out on your life. Sing the praises of the Lamb who truly would rather die than live without *you.* And when you are too tired to dance or sing or proclaim His mercy any longer, then fall on your face and join the millions in Revelation 5 with the cry: *"Worthy is the Lamb that was slain!"*

How do I live this life as a young Christian? How do I stand as a rebel of grace? Never forget what you just heard.

Never believe that your life is about merit or works or you.

Never misunderstand the commands to live for God. Never see your deeds of righteousness to be a merit badge to show God. He will one day look at all the works that you have done since conversion, and He will nod, but only if they were done through Christ (Phil. 4:13). They will not earn you one ounce of His mercy, His favor, or His love though because, guess what, you know—you already have all.

15

Liberty

So Christ has really set us free!
Galatians 5:1 NLT

The man stood by himself. Gazing out through the steel bars, he saw the multitude of citizens swarming about like a hive of angry bees. His sandy, unkempt hair fell in his face, almost concealing his pale, blue eyes. He was extremely thin. He wore no shirt and through the scarred tissue on his back one could easily make out his rib cage and spinal column. This man *was* emaciated, possibly to the point of starvation.

Grimly, he rotated his bony wrists, attempting to alleviate the itch that irritated the flesh beneath the iron shackles. How many times had he counted the links in these chains? How many times had he sat in a barred wagon just like this one? How many times had his number been called and a bid been made upon his head, only to

be transferred from one owner to another? How many
more times would this go on before his strength ran out?
His current bondage seemed remarkably similar to every
previous slavery. He was starving for nourishment. His
body ached from beatings. His tongue was parched and
his lips cracked. Blood—dried over the course of several
days—had accumulated at the edges of his mouth. How
much more could he take?

And yet today was a day like so many before it. He
had been roughly awakened that morning. Some of
the stronger slaves had been tossed a shirt to improve
their appearance. These men would go for a higher sale.
However, this slave's master considered him to be of no
worth whatsoever so the luxury of a shirt was not pro-
vided. One look at the feeble man and a less than discern-
ing eye could perceive that it would take some expense to
restore him to heath and strength. Such financial sacrifice was rarely, if ever, bestowed upon a slave. Therefore,
the owner had decided that for this particular slave any
offer would be readily accepted.

The prison carriage ground to a halt, sending the dust
circling upward in small dust devils. The thin slave choked
on the filthy powder as it filled the wagon. His light blue
eyes blinked back tears. Reaching up to rub those eyes
only brought a fresh sense of pain. Exhaustion tormented
the poor man. He swallowed hard—his throat a trail of
raw flesh. Keys jangled, the lock clanked free, and the
barred door on the back on the wagon swung open. Fresh
waves of the city dust swept in through the opening, and
the muggy heat almost suffocated the prisoners.

The stronger slaves sat near the exit. This had been
the design of the foreman who knew that the first slaves

to step through the door ought to be the most impressive to the crowd of prospective buyers. Owing to this fact, the last to exit the wagon was that withered man with the light blue eyes. He had to be partially assisted by another slave, for his legs were too feeble to carry his skinny frame. With both his assistant's wrists under his left arm, the man leaned on a cane in his right hand and staggered forward. He was fully aware that few eyes were on him, and those who were looked upon him in disgust. The starving slave was also fully aware that should he fail to be sold on this day he would be put to death by his own current master to cut financial losses. He had seen it happen before—a poor wretch, whom no one purchased, was either left to rot outside the slave quarters or beaten by his captors until the fierce blows shattered his frail limbs and crushed the life out of his heaving chest. With these frightening images filling his head, the poor slave attempted to erect his frail form.

Slowly, the slaves proceeded up to the platform to join the many others who stood in shackles. Very few of the bound men gazed out at the throngs of people. Most of them glared at the rough boards beneath their bare feet. Not the frail slave though. Having ever so gradually made his way up the steps and onto the scaffold, he let his eyes sweep across the masses, hoping, praying for a ray of hope. Was there truly anyone who would purchase him? With these thoughts running through the mind of the weary slave, the auction began.

The auctioneer flamboyantly approached the podium. His clothes were fashionable, yet wrinkled, matching his dirty face and unruly hair. Spreading his arms as if in a sure stroke of grandeur, the man's clear voice rang out hushing the crowd. He treated the platform as his palace. Indeed, he did control the atmosphere and his manners and strong vocals demanded attention.

Charismatically, the auctioneer brought one bond-servant forward at a time. He would yell out a price, someone would raise his or her hand, and then the incessant chatter would begin.

"Fifty pence, who will give me a hundred? I see a hundred; who will give me two? Two, how about two-fifty?" And so the auction went. As each transaction was completed, the buyer would stride up to the scaffold, and the exchanging of one set of chains for another would occur. As always, the strongest of the slaves were sold first. Next came the slaves who were still in good health, and finally the...finally the weak and the physically ill. Those with handicaps fetched a small sum. Amidst these transactions those who were interested would come forward to examine the sickly prisoners. They would then make a wager—some for just a few pence—and if no one outbid them then the slaves would be sold for the small amount declared.

The time finally came. Of all the prisoners to be sold he was the last. There he stood, alone, leaning on his cane. The stick could barely support him and at any time he feared that he might fall to the splintered wood beneath his soiled toes.

The auctioneer glanced at the feeble and sickly slave and did not wonder why he had put off this one till the last. The very sight of the man was repulsive. His cheekbones were sunken, every limb quivered, every visible bone was pronounced. He was pale, extremely pale, and his features held almost an ashen hue to them.

Truly, he appeared to be a walking corpse.

The only light of life seemed to resonate from those light blue eyes, but that was all, and masters did not purchase slaves on the basis of their eyes. *This one will not be sold today*, the auctioneer mused under his breath. However, owing to the obligations of his occupation, he had to announce every bondservant and allow the mass of people to reject him.

Many, upon seeing the lone remaining slave on the platform, scowled and turn to meander on their way. Others seemed to chuckle at the idea that someone would actually pay anything for this man, or half a man. The sun was setting and now the multitude began to think on other things, such as what they would be eating tonight or who would be in their company.

Dreading the inevitable, the auctioneer sighed. He had to do it, better to get it over with. The thin prisoner could see the hesitation in the face of the auctioneer. He could discern the mood of the crowd. He could detect no sign of hope. Perhaps it would be better to die than to live.

The voice of the auctioneer split the now evening air one last time. "Who, who desires this man?" Never throughout the course of that afternoon had the auctioneer hesitated. The crowd caught it, as did the poor wretch hunched over his cane. A murmur swept through the crowd. No bid came. No one strode toward the platform. To all, it was apparent that the slave was of no worth. There was, indeed, no good thing to be desired of him.

"Come now," the proclamation rang out, "who will buy this man? Do I hear five pence? Five?"

No one moved.

"Three pence? Who will give me three?"

Still nothing. The crowd was growing bored and many continued to leave the vicinity.

The auctioneer glanced down at this frail slave's master. The master sternly glared back at the man behind the podium and held up one finger. The auctioneer grimaced. "All right, folks...one! Who will give me one penny? Do I hear one? Just one?"

A horse neighed nearby. A young child cried. Dogs barked. Still no one moved.

"Will no one take this slave?" The final query sounded like the death sentence for the humiliated slave. His lip quivered. A tear crept into his eye. No one desired him, not one. He was indeed worthless. He was the off scouring, the very worst of the worst. A ball of grief had arisen in his throat. His knees could bear the strain no longer. Incapable of standing on his own, the desperate man collapsed on his cane. The cane could not stand though, not in light of the man's weight, and thus the slave collapsed on the scaffold. The rough wood bit into his hand. Blood seeped from fresh cuts. His mouth dry, his face lifeless, his hands empty—the poor, helpless man lay there under the scrutiny of his master and the condemning crowd. The cane still rested firmly in the prisoner's gaunt hand. The people scoffed brazenly. The auctioneer looked down in disgust. The master mounted the platform to lord above the fallen man.

The crowd now watched curiously. Few doubted what the master would declare. Brashly the master declared through a voice laced with cynicism, "This man is of no value! Let him be put to death!"

There it was. The death toll had sounded. Far too feeble to struggle, the prisoner saw the tormentors approaching to carry him away to his death. Just as they reached the platform, however, a voice like the sound of a trumpet resounded across the crowd.

"Ten thousand talents!"

A gasp ascended from the throng of citizens. The tormentors approaching the scaffold whirled to see from where the voice had come. The master peered into the crowd. The auctioneer cleared his throat. "Uh, what was that?"

"I will give ten thousand talents for the slave!" The voice carried with it a tone of authority.

"Who are you?" the master cried. "Surely you are insane! Why should you desire this scum?"

A man stepped through the crowd, dressed in robes of royal color. He had strong servants standing on both sides of him, anxious to obey any command given. From his position, the auctioneer began to recollect where these two servants had come from. At one time, they, too, had been miserable wretches, lying helpless upon this very scaffold. And now, look at them.

The master standing over the fallen slave, however, had eyes only for the bidder. He knew the man clothed in royal splendor. This was the lord of the city. He demanded and deserved the utmost respect and honor. Yet for some reason, he desired this heap of worthless humanity. Why?

The lord completed his trek to the platform and then mounted the steps, his servants at his heels. It was then that he spoke, his voice lucid and authoritative. "I will give ten thousand silver talents for this man."

The astonishment was apparent on the faces of all. Not only was this powerless slave being bought, but for an exuberant sum. The master was confounded. "Why?" he muttered. "Why do you desire this...this...?"

"Because I do," came the simple reply.

"But what good do you see in him?"

"None, but I can change that," the new master stated boldly.

"For such a lucrative amount though." the auctioneer chimed in. "Why not purchase him for two pence?"

"Because I desire to show just how much I would give for this slave." The lord's eyes shone. "Demand a higher price and I shall gladly give it."

No one said anything else. The lord reached within his robe, withdrew a large, velvet, money purse, and dropped it at the feet of the old master. He then handed his scepter to one of his servants, and kneeling beside the fallen slave, he pried the cane from those bony fingers, tossing it away forever. Then stoking the grizzled hair of the slave he smiled. "Welcome home, my son."

The lord's two servants beamed. The crowds simply gawked in amazement and wonder. No one could understand. How could this lord care for such a person and call him his son? It was undeniably a wonder of wonders.

With keys in hand, the lord unlocked the chains, handed them back to the previous owner, and did not replace them with new irons of his own. He then rapped his own royal arms around the fragile form of this slave, lifting him to his feet. Taking his cloak from his won shoulders, the lord draped it upon the shaking frame of the purchased prisoner.

At the removal of the chains and the mere touch of the lord, the slave felt new life course through his veins. He breathed the fresh air, as he leaned on his new master. He felt the love flowing throughout his being for this his lord. He knew that from this moment on he would gladly do whatever the lord asked, so great was his admiration and appreciation for the gift that has just been applied for him.

The crowd parted as the lord—supporting his new *son*—passed through them. The slave turned into a son. None understood, though some now remembered witnessing this transaction occur before.

Climbing into his beautiful carriage, the lord nodded to his servants who called to the horses. The white steeds moved in unison, carrying the lord and the slave away. The next time the masses would see this slave, they fully knew that he would be strong and healthy like the other servant-sons. And as for the lord, they would see him again on the next auction day.

A Privilege to Serve

What a majestic portrait of grace—a brilliant display of the love of God. He chose to sacrifice so that we as slaves could be declared *the children of God.* This story teaches remarkable truths about the salvation of Christ.

As you may have easily discerned, we are those helplessly, weakened slaves that have nothing but a life or worthlessness to offer God (John 8:34). Desperately seeking deliverance, all that fills our spiritual vision is an empty vacuum of lust and selfish desire. While we are "strong" in our own eyes, we arrogantly assume that we could make it through, despite the fact that we are only being transferred from one bondage to another (Rom. 1:21). We have to come to a point of total weakness—where we have no hope remaining. Seeing our own inadequacies and falling desperately toward destruction, everything within us cries for salvation, and suddenly God breaks through the crowds. Even though our former master, Satan, has pronounced a curse upon us, Christ shatters the chains through His priceless gift.

Just as in the story, He chooses to redeem us (Gal. 4:5), to buy us back for Himself. Unworthy, unwanted, there we lie clutching tightly to the cane of our good works and bound by the chains of our iniquities. Just like the cane in the story, our works can never support us (Titus 3:5). Rotting with sin, we crumble upon our deeds, crashing downward (Isa. 64:6). Yet the Lord comes, and with the love of a father, He casts away our works (Eph. 2:8-9)—proving the worthlessness of them—so we can glory only in Him (Eph. 1:14). He then eradicates the debt against us, with that velvet purse of His blood, that precious blood (Heb. 1:3), that blood that atones for sinful men forever (Heb. 10:14). And then in a glorious sweep, He removes the chains of sin, casting them as far away from us as the east is from the west (Col. 2:13-14; Ps. 103:12). Finally, here we stand, supported only by the Person of Christ, dressed in his cloak of righteousness (2 Cor. 5:21).

Surely, we will, having seen this display of what Christ did for our salvation, surrender to love and willingly serve our Master eternally. It is our pleasure and privilege to do so in response to His grace.

You know what the coolest part of this story is? Although the crowd of spectators does not understand our redemption and reconciliation to God, they admire the Master who indeed bought us with a price, and therefore, all the glory goes to Him alone.

You did nothing to deserve your salvation, young friend. Now you can do nothing to preserve that salvation. Salvation is given and sustained through Jesus Christ. Why He did it will remain a partial mystery to us, but we can be sure that it was not based upon anything we did, or will do. It is all about His grace.

Your life and mine...we are trophies of grace.

That grace brought us to Him and that grace will transform us into passionate pursuers of God (Rom. 8:29)!

Here is my extreme message to you, friend—young or old: If you have accepted Jesus as your life's Savior then you are free! This is because God has forgiven you on the basis of the cross. He has vigorously snatched you from the chains of evil and condemnation under the law and has set you in the light. *He has delivered us from the domain of darkness and transferred us into the kingdom of His beloved Son, in whom we have redemption, the forgiveness of sins* (Col. 1:13-14)! What is Paul saying here? He is proclaiming that freedom has been purchased for *us* through the blood of Jesus, and He has forgiven us for all the sin we have committed.

Does this not astonish you? Does this extreme display

of grace not blow you away? Does it not spark within you a desire to stand for Him, to tell others of this gift, to hold up a hand and say no to traditionalism and empty philosophy? If so, then you are beginning to understand the rebellion of grace! It begins here, with liberation.

Perhaps this just seems orthodox, standard. It is something that we have read in the Bible on a few occasions. We know we are free, we have nibbled at the concept a little here and there, but no more, friend. Now is the time to come to terms with the fact that I am a son or daughter of the most high God of eternity, and I am forever free to live! Bite into a juicy piece of this freedom. Let it sit on your tongue and taste the sweet flavor of grace. Don't be content to nibble any longer; instead take an entire mouthful of liberation and live.

16

Life

But God being rich in mercy because of the great love
with which he loved us, even when we were dead in
our trespasses, made us alive together with Christ.
Ephesians 2:4–5

"So why even live for God? If we are forgiven of every
future sin then why worry about holiness or surrender?
Let's just live in grace!"

If these are your comments after reading the previous chapter, my friend, then you need to go back to
page one and start all over. You need to read Paul's reply
to such a pagan attitude in Romans 6:1–2. You need
to overlook consequence and even commandment. You
need to gaze upon that Man of righteousness once more.
Look into those eyes. Feel His heart beat for you. Watch
the spike make a gruesome incision through the tender
skin of His wrists. See the bloodied face...the distorted

body...the limbs quivering in agony...Hear Him whisper, "Father...forgive . . ." And then, once more, witness His grand declaration, "It is finished!" Then after seeing all this yet again, perhaps your question will not be, *Why live for God?* Rather your passion will be...

I get to live for God!

This should be my response to His love and His redemption. We—like the slave on the platform—were sentenced to a very, horrible end. Yet Christ stepped in, and by showing His sacrifice of love—the blood of His broken body—the Father declared us to be free.

That, my friend, is the most amazing love story ever. That is why I wrote the tale of the slave turned to a son. That is why God—that very God of mercy—included in His inspired volume of love, a wonderfully remarkable story of a woman caught in a despicable act of iniquity and forgiven, by the mercy of a Savior.

Why did God decide to do this for *us?* Why does it bring Him glory? Why *us* when everything is about God? My friend, I have no idea. But though it is a mystery of mercy, it ought to leave us everyday crying out in ardent praise for that mercy! Paul said it best in 2 Corinthians 5:14, *The love of Christ is what drives my life!* (Author's paraphrase.) No, I don't have to serve or live for God, but because of His blazing love for me, it is my privileged pleasure to live for His glory! I get to pursue God with everything in me! And if I don't, it is merely proof that I haven't really tasted grace.

Each morning as my eyes flutter open I ought to look upon and savor the reality of the Savior's love. I ought to dance in the liberation of His grace throughout my day. I ought to talk of His wonders with renewed vigor at each fresh encounter He brings along my path. I ought to continually bow in solemn, sacred worship at the brilliance of His Person...

and with joyful ecstasy, celebrate the beauty of His passion for me.

Was this not the heart-wrenching cry of Paul in Galatians 2:20? *The life I now live in the flesh I live by the faith of the Son of God.* In the previous verse, Paul claims that because of Christ's death on Calvary, he is free from the law so now he can really live for God. Why is this? Is it something Paul felt like he *had* to do? No. It was merely a reaction to understanding what God had gone through for *him. I live for Christ because He loved me and gave Himself for me!*

It is with this attitude of worshipful amazement that you will truly begin to understand how to live the Christian life as a teen or adult. It is in *response* to His love for *us* that we live.

My friend, you have been given a life of freedom! Now live it.

17

The *pursuit* of God

Whatever we do, it is because Christ's love controls us.
2 Corinthians 5:14 NLT

By this point perhaps your head is swimming and all you want is an easy chair and an *Advil.* Though few of us would readily admit it—because after all, that would hurt our pride—this is quite a bit to take in. The questions are, no doubt, beginning to blaze like artillery in a hot battle.

So, Aaron, you're saying that we don't have to please God, but we have to please God? Yes, that sounds confusing, I'll confess. So let me establish the truth with extreme simplicity. Our purpose is not to win souls, read our Bibles, go to church, help widows, or perform any number of actions to please God. However...

if you have no desire to do any of these things your spiritual thermometer could be reading zero, showing that you are still lifeless.

The works mentioned above are not to merit salvation, grace, the smile of God, or His pleasure. They are merely the overflow of a life that has been filled with grace.

It should not be our duty to please God, and I will say it again with finality: nothing I can do as a true child of God will ever forfeit His favor or His smile. There, it is said, but do not run off on me now. This truth of grace is often distorted, and more professing believers will burn in eternal hell for an improper understanding of this doctrine, leading to an immoral, unregenerate life.

Love and Live

The woman caught in adultery in Chapter Two was not just to reveal to you the forgiveness of Christ. His love, mercy, and unconditional forgiveness are awesome, yes, but we must dig even deeper than this.

Christians of today often see this story as a liberty to live any way they desire. *There is no reason to kill our sinful passions. We have been forgiven all. Christ has looked upon us, as He looked upon the adulteress, and declared, "I do not condemn you." Therefore, with every crime forgiven and eternity secure we can shrug off the commands to be "holy because I am holy" or "live for the glory of Christ." Those orders are transformed into Divine suggestions, and if we choose to ignore them, electing a life of wickedness or just pure apathy, that's okay, because, hey, we're forgiven, right?*

Wrong!

We are like the adulteress not condemned, but also—like the adulteress—we are to *go* and *leave* our life of sin!

Okay, so here is the deal, you might think. *Now that we have been forgiven and conversion has occurred...now that I am a child of God...now that I have been saved by grace, I must live a life of holiness. I must radiate holiness. No, we can't lose our salvation because it was given to us by grace, but we can lose the blessings, favor, and that burning love of God through what we say, do, or think. So we must erect standards and convictions in our lives to keep us from forfeiting His heavenly approval of us, right?*

Once again, wrong!

Consequently, the seesaw totters back and forth. One extreme is *legalism*—setting up rules and works as means of attaining spiritually and right standing with God; the other extreme is *libertinism*—feeling that grace gives me the right to live however I choose.

So the answer is found in the middle? The thought finally connects with you. *A false view of grace leading to lawlessness if wrong, but so is a false view of the law leading to legalism. Consequently the answer lies somewhere in the center. For you and I to understand and live the Christian life we must maintain "balance" on the seesaw between libertinism and legalism, right?*

If this is where your mind has taken you, you are, once more, absolutely wrong!

The answer is not balance between two false concepts. Take the Judaizers in Galatians who taught that obeying the law brought the favor of God, and the libertines in Jude who knew that they possessed the favor of God and therefore could live for their own desires. Combining them together what do you create? A solid, passionate believer? No way! You have just formed a monster with a completely distorted view of grace and works...or someone completely confused.

No, the answer is found not in the center of the equation between these two erroneous extremes. Rather the answer is found in *Someone* far, far above these philosophies of carnal reasoning (Eph. 1:20–21). The answer is Christ. Yes, it is as simple as that.

Far above the playground filled with seesaws of all wrong philosophies, blazes the cross!

A walk of holiness is important...but it is just another one of those spokes in the bike wheel. The hub is our constant—and that is Christ Jesus (Col. 2:8).

Making Sense of it all

Perhaps you are a young person—or just young at heart—and you feel totally worthless. Maybe you have committed the most heinous of all sins in your mind. Your friends, parents, or spouse won't forgive you. You sense that a raging forest-fire has swept through your being, destroying all that was once pure and right. You feel as if a herd of charging stallions has pounded across your soul leaving nothing but an empty cavern of crushed dreams and fleshly ruins. You have abused your mind or body, and now your spirit lies helplessly in forlorn dread. No life seems to rush through your being, and to others you seem a bottomless well of useless decay. Not worthy to be forgiven?

Hey, neither was the adulteress; yet Christ Jesus, the very God of Heaven looked into her eyes and spoke those words: "I don't condemn you!"

If you are apart from Christ today, attempting to live life on your own and you just happened to see the title of this work and you gave it a shot—that, my friend, was no accident. God chose for you to read this. He is conveying to you through His love letter, we call the Bible, that He is a God of forgiveness. No matter what you have done if you feel Him drawing you to that place of brokenness over your sin, and you through the simple gift of faith confess your sin to Him, you will be forgiven all. Yes, Christianity in its true, biblical form is just that simple.

I am forgiven and you can be too. And, if you have trusted Christ, you are free as well (Rom. 8:2). Your salvation can never be lost because it is not your salvation to lose. It is God's salvation and you are His child!

However, that freedom for the woman caught in adultery was not a license to do whatever she desired in her flesh to do (Rom. 6:1–2; Acts 10:43). No. Instead, because she had been forgiven so much and set free from the clutches of iniquity, her immediate desire no doubt was to worship the Lamb!

That is the purpose of the story of the miserable slave in Chapter Fifteen. Place yourself on that scaffold. No hope...no salvation...only death approaching...but suddenly a true Savior breaks forth and not only does He pay the price for your freedom, but He adopts you into His family. How could you not forever *yearn* to live for Him?

What could possibly keep you from loving Him and out of that love would flow passionate service (2 Cor. 5:14)?

When set up as a duty the Christian life does seem like a walk of merit...and that is where many go wrong. However—on the opposite end—it is not a free-for-all, self-liberating license to join in the total elation of the world around us...and that is where far more are falling off the plateau of grace-based, biblical rationalism today. In an ill-fated, ill-logical twist of the truth, ministers, youth leaders, college students, and teenagers by the droves are racing to the attractive glories of a God who saves us from hell but certainly not from sin!

But is this at all truth? Did the Son of God step down into this decaying world of human depravity to merely hold our head above the slime of Satan's toys, while we muse in them? Or did Christ—as the Conquering Lamb of the Most High—reach down and actually rescue us from the sewage that held us in lifeless captivity so that we can vigorously pursue God (2 Cor. 5:15)?

My young companion, Jesus Christ is our Rescuer. He saved us and called us to a life of holiness as we walk with Him (Heb. 12:14; 2 Tim.1:9)...and our pursuit of holiness is guided by His grace (Heb. 12:15). Was it not the angel of the Lord who told the Virgin Mary that she would have a Son who would be a Savior *from* sin (Matt. 1:21)? To me that sounds very much like an *active* Redeemer who actually liberates people from the bondage of sin!

As we have already witnessed, to us who are in the blessed hope of Christ, there is no condemnation. Forever, we are made right with God and no one can ever level a charge against us (Rom. 8:33). But, for those of us who are in Christ Jesus, we *will walk* after the Spirit and not after our flesh (Rom. 8:2). That is our identification.

"All right, Aaron!" you cry. "First you say that we do not have to please God; now you say we must live for Him. I do not know how to live the Christian life at all, and as a young person, honestly, I am too confused and bewildered to care!"

If that is your attitude presently (or if not) allow me to repeat this very simple truth to you one more time: we do not have to gain the favor of God by living for Him. We *already have* the special favor of God through the Savior's sacrifice. However, as we meditate on this truth, our heart *should* pump with a renewed vigor to serve and live for Him out of love! Don't you see? The Christian life is not a life of duty as we strive to measure up! Rather, the Christian life for you, young person or adult, is understanding that the mercy of God through the death and resurrection of the Son of God has made you perfect in the eyes of God, and therefore...

our response to beholding that incredible love will be a life of passionate dedication to our Divine Lover!

Do not piddle away in an action-based existence. Rather live in a life of reactionary passion as a rebel of mercy, looking at those two pieces of wood on which all of your sins were crushed (1 Peter 2:24).

18

Drunk on *grace!*

Do not be led away by diverse and strange teachings,
for it is good for the heart to be strengthened by grace…
Hebrews 13:9

Consuming thoughts

We have all been in love at one time or another…or at least thought we were. Some of us poor, hopeless romantics believe we will never find true love. Others of us believe we have found it on more than one occasion. Everyone—even if they don't want a relationship or a commitment—wants to be in love. For me, it is no different.

Her name was Angie. Wherever she might be now, if she picks up this book and reads it she will laugh. She was a cheerleader for my high school team when I was just a freshman. I had recently grown nine inches in the span of a single year, and going from a five foot six inch, starting, junior varsity point guard to a six foot three inch, varsity, "powerless" forward was awkward enough for me. Moppy hair, a mouth full of metal, and a shy demeanor definitely did not assist in my social development. I liked girls. Okay, I loved girls, but no one outside of my family would have guessed it because I never—*ever*—talked to them. They scared me speechless. Give me a room full of guys and I was the life of the party. However, put just one girl in the room and I was silent as the grave.

Maybe it was torture...or chastisement, but at the age of 14 I saw Angie for the first time—a cute blonde, with a big smile and lively eyes. It was "puppy love" at first sight...but only for me. For two years I don't think Angie realized I actually existed. Yea, she was a cheerleader for *my* team, and I was a starter who averaged double figures in points and rebounds...but I was infatuated with an absolute stranger. The thought never pushed its way into my dense, teenage skull that if I ever wanted a chance with her I might in reality have to speak to her. So for two long years my crush grew, and though speaking a combined four sentences to her over the course of those basketball seasons, I simply *knew* that destiny had designed us for one another. Every morning when I awoke from sleep, my first thought was of that blonde-haired cheerleader. Throughout each day, I would hopelessly gawk at her picture, which ironically one of her ex-boyfriends had given me.

Yea, I was ridiculous, and it is still embarrassing to share these secrets with you, my reader. Every night I would cry out to the God I still had not come to know to please show Angie that we were meant to be together. Every moment was consumed by thoughts of her...until one day I discovered that she had moved away and that maybe—just possibly—we were not destined to be together after all.

Consuming Actions

It was three years later, as a fresh-faced, immature high school graduate that I dove into my first romantic relationship. Now not only were all of my thoughts consumed by "love" but so were my actions. I did things for this girl all the time. She was in every thought I had and every act I carried out.

I'll never forget the day I wired her a dozen long-stem red roses. The fee was exorbitant, but to me, it was nothing. I "loved" this girl so every "inconvenience" was transformed into a privilege. Every obligation was now a chance for me to demonstrate my affection for her even further. No, never in all those months did I feel obligated to actually *do* things for that young woman. It was always my joyful opportunity to do for her because of the overwhelming feelings I felt for her. No price was too high to pay. No duty too hard to carry out. But hey, after all, I was "in love."

How much more should we love Him?

Hopefully, in these two insane stories of misconceived affection you are beginning to discern my point. It is never a drudgery to think on a crush or to buy things for a girlfriend or boyfriend. Whatever that special one asks for, you girls happily carry it out because you love him. Whatever she desires, guys, you gladly buy it—if you can afford it—or do it because you have passions running through you that can't be ignored. Those feelings transform even the most unwanted tasks into love-sick privileges.

So it should be with our love for God! If we truly love Him as we say, then it should not be an arduous chore to live for Him (2 Cor. 5:14). Whatever He desires we should be willing to do it because He loved us enough to sacrifice! If you say that you want His salvation, but don't want any part of loving Him, then you will die without Christ and spend an eternity under His wrath (1 Cor. 16:22). It's simple, friend; if you love Him, live for Him.

Getting Drunk on the Good Stuff

On several occasions I have seen them staggering down the boardwalk at Pensacola Beach, screaming obnoxiously at anyone happening to stroll by. Frequently, obscenities fall from their lips. Blatant mood swings are exhibited. Displays of heightened emotion become the norm.

Alcoholic intoxication is crippling individuals of this generation. What's the danger? It lies in the truth that once a person, young or old, has consumed too much alcohol, the drink takes control of the mind, and the body succumbs to the liquor's commands. Therefore, everything that a drunken individual does is governed by the power of that drink. It is not a choice people make to allow the alcohol to control them; instead, the power of the drink simply takes the control and the individual submits to that power.

Young person, this is how true Christianity works! In the same way, we are to be so intoxicated with Christ that the power of Christ controls our life! That is the crux of

Paul's cry in 2 Corinthians 5: that I have drunk so deeply of grace that now I am drunk of the very Spirit of God! He is Who controls me. His mercy is the reason I live my life the way I do. No, I am not *allowing* Him to manage my course of direction; instead, I am simply surrendering my existence to the power of one Almighty Creator so that through my life I may bring Him glory!

Young friend, now is the time to drink deeply of mercy! It is now that your life should become saturated with Christ! This is what I call us to—an existence of intoxication with

passionate grace!

The most effective means of defeating evil is to be drunk on truth! Delve into His Word; drink of the revelation that He has breathed out for you! Consume it, and after a while, when your heart is saturated with the love of His cross and the beauty of His blood, the power of grace will overwhelm and ultimately control your thoughts and your actions! This is what it means to be intoxicated with grace. It will not take place with a gaze focused on stamping out evil, instead it will only occur when we, as young zealots with eyes fixated on the miracle of Golgotha, begin to understand and marvel at the mystery of mercy.

That Life of Holiness

Having witnessed His love and grace toward *us*, a love beyond all measure should begin to burn within us, driving us to live for Him, enjoy Him, and bathe in His glory every day. That love will grow into a full-blown passion, and soon, as we walk through our Christian pilgrimage, everything we do for Christ Jesus will be an inexpressible delight and we will unconsciously stand as rebels *of* God.

Sure we will still fail at times, but the pattern of self gratification will slowly begin to dissolve. Why? Why give up our sinful desires to live a life of righteousness? Is it to gain favor with God? No. It is because we love Him so much that our desires to this world are dying. We don't want to delve into things that He hates. Our desire is His desire. Was that not what the apostle Paul stated was the repercussion of the cross in Galatians 6:14? *Because of that cross,* he writes, *my interest in this world died long ago, and the world's interest in me is long dead* (NLT).

It is interesting that before dealing with the Christian walk in many of his epistles, Paul outlines the conquering quest of Christ over death and hell. In Romans Paul reveals the depths of our depravity, the weight of the Savior's love, and the bliss of true reconciliation to God the Father, before ever touching our personal lives after that point of reconciliation. For eleven chapters the Gospel of Christ is gloriously displayed...what He actually accomplished for us...and then finally in verse one of Chapter Twelve Paul declares, *I appeal to you therefore, brothers, by the mercies of God, to present your bodies as a living sacrifice, holy and acceptable to God, which is your spiritual worship.* Paul stresses this rational service to God after the grand exaltation at the end of Chapter Eleven. He shows the brilliance of God's mind, the riches of His wisdom, and the glory that belongs to Him forever. He brings us to true worship—a surrendered life—but only on the basis of His mercies. Paul finishes with the words, *Is this really too much after all He has done for you* (NLT)?

To the Romans believers who received this epistle, the response to all the love displayed in chapters one through eleven was clear. He loved us when we were haters of God (5:8). He suffered for our vile actions against His own decree of righteousness (4:25). He actively brought criminals into eternal friendship with the Father (5:10). This was not for people who were distant to the Romans. Christ actually underwent this for them. He actively bore their sins!

My friend, this, Christ did for *you!* If you have believed on Him, then it is *you* for whom Jesus died. His blood has bought for *you* eternal life (Heb. 9:12). His death has delivered *you* from the clutches of sin (1 Peter 1:18–19). His own righteousness has brought *you* into holy standing before God (Rom. 5:9). You see, this was not done for some person out there whom you will never meet. It is not abstract theology; it is intensely personal! This wonderful work of redemption was wrought out for *you!*

When we look upon the disfigured, bloody body of a dying Man in Chapter Four, what we are to see is not a human being who lived in the first century. Rather we *must* see the God who suffered...the God who was blasphemed...the God who ordained His creation to strike the face of the Lamb...the God who separated Himself from His Father for a brief moment in time...so He could take *your* sin upon His back and die for *you* (Isaiah 53:11)! Now we answer once again the query set forth in the opening chapters: why did the Father send His Son to this earth, born into human flesh and subjecting Himself to His own law (Gal. 4:4)? The answer is simple, yet for eternity we should never get over the beauty of this Divine declaration. He did all this...*to redeem us* (4:5)!

And it is with these thoughts of God's love blazing in the minds of the Roman readers that Paul then declares to them, *I now appeal to you, brothers, by this mercy of God, that you present your bodies as a living sacrifice.*

The obvious response to a sacrifice of Divine worth to bring enemies of God into eternal fellowship with Him is worshipful, personal sacrifice!

Following up his statements of all that God has done in blessing us (1:3), choosing us to be His children (1:4), adopting us into His family (1:5), redeeming us with His blood (1:7), giving us a divine inheritance (1:11), making us His completion (1:23), making us alive (2:5), reconciling us to Himself (2:6), granting to us eternal life (2:7), gifting us with a new will and ability to believe (2:8), bringing us near by His blood (2:13), making us members of His family (2:19), and bestowing upon us the competence to understand the brilliance of His love in order that we may be full of God Himself (3:19), is it any wonder that Paul declares, *I urge you to walk in a manner worthy of the calling to which you have been called* (Eph. 4:1)? This was no drudgery for the converts in Ephesus. It was not a tedious chore, this life as a Christian. Each hardship they endured for the sake of the Gospel; each time they were mocked, they remembered the sacrifice of *their* God and valued those times as a privilege. After all, they, too, were first-century rebels.

You see, young person, it is absolutely necessary for

you and I to meditate on the cross work of Christ before we will ever begin to understand life as twenty-first century believers. It is absolutely essential for you to gaze upon the suffering that the Son of God willingly chose to go through for you. And it is absolutely essential that you make His redemption on that cross of brutality the center of your very life. It is for this reason that I wrote this book.

19

Don't Let it *Die*

Let your roots grow down into him and draw up
nourishment from him, so you will grow in faith…
Colossians 2:7 NLT

Catadupa, Jamaica, July 2005

It was July. I grabbed my guitar, summoning our mission team to worship. We were in the interior mountains of Jamaica. Our work had gone well. Leading a Vacation Bible School for children with an attention span that lasted through a *Jolly Rancher* had been a struggle but well worth it. With the construction projects complete and our labor on the island coming to a close, I had chosen to gather our team together for one last time of praise in the mountains.

This night was different from the others though. Instead of meeting inside the "chapel" with our Bibles and songbooks, I decided to assemble outside. We all congregated in a small half-finished elementary school. The concrete floor had been poured making it easy for the girls to spread blankets to sit on. The walls had been partially erected and stood anywhere from four to six feet tall all the way around. The building rested on the side of one mountain, offering a spectacular view of the valley and another mountain range. The sun had just set and dusk was approaching as I addressed the group.

I can't remember exactly what I spoke on that night. Honestly, no one present at the time probably can. I know it had something to do with Job's reply to God's decree and how instead of answering the accusations God merely showed Job the power of I AM. We prayed for God to show us Himself and by the time I strummed the first chord a spirit of adoration had settled upon each individual in that unfinished school house.

The words of familiar praise songs flowed from our lips, but for once, they weren't just words. Tears began to blur the eyes of many young people. Hearts pumped with passion for the God of all wonders. Soon enough the singing had turned to cries of Christ-exalting worship! No one cared if they were on pitch. No one cared if I missed a chord.

All that mattered was that God had chosen to show up, and not one person could deny it!

By now the sky overhead was a black canopy, sprinkled with a million pin-points of light, each one attesting to the greatness of our God! Clouds filled the valley below. The heat of the day had dissipated and the cool breeze now calmly whisked across faces that gazed heavenward. Shooting stars blazed through the night sky.

As I opened my eyes to glance around I saw young men, hands lifted to Heaven, weeping freely. Young woman, eyes sealed shut, and arms outstretched as if soaking in the reality of God. Others knelt with heads bowed. Still others lay flat on their back gazing up at the Creator's canopy. The moment was breathtaking! It seemed to last only an instant, when in reality we were out on the side of that mountain for hours.

Even now, several months later, I look back at that blip on the timeline of history and I want to go back. I long to relive it. My desire is to breathe God Himself! To feel His presence so real and personal to *me!* I wish I could go back to that moment, and I wish somehow, I could press pause.

Your "Pause" Button

There are times in all of our lives that we desire to hit the "pause" button. Where we don't want the moment—whatever it might be—to end. We wish it could somehow go on indefinitely. The reason for this is simple. We live for the phenomenal, and the phenomenal is rarely something you can create. It is something that just happens.

What was it for you? What instance did you desire to hold onto?

Perhaps it was your fifteen minutes of fame. Standing in the spotlight, you stared out at the "adoring fans" and felt those chills ascending your backbone.

Maybe it was on the athletic field, guys. You stood at the plate, lined a sharp drive to left-center, and as the ball hit the alley, you streaked past second and dove into third. Your adrenaline felt like it would blast out of your chest. Your triple had cleared the bases giving your team the lead late in the ballgame. Rising to your feet and dusting off your pants, you gazed at the celebration in your dugout as the chant of your name resounded from the packed bleachers.

Possibly, for you girls, it was just sitting on the hood of a car. The sun was dipping on the horizon sending a blanket of warmth across your face. Your eyes were drawn into the gaze of that one...*the* one you had secretly been in love with for three years. Now it was just the two of you, and this moment...this moment you wished would never end.

Whatever the circumstance, we have all had times like these mentioned above. Times we wanted nothing more than to forever bask in the moment at hand. Times where we wanted to press "pause."

Pause at the Cross

With the conclusion of the last chapter we have our springboard into the final leg of our journey. How do we actually live as a rebel of grace, maintaining a burning zeal for God? Just as the previous chapter stated...it must be *in Christ!* We gain true passion and maintain that passion by gazing at, meditating on, and getting to know Him!

We get so caught up in the how-to's of Christianity that we forget our Substance. We seek ways to maintain a clear outflow, while neglecting the Source. Books today are sadly pointing us to methods that might work, instead of the Savior who will *never* fail!

Laid out clearly in the epistle to the congregation at Colosse is the "secret" to the Christian life. It is not to be holy or love others or read the Bible a designated amount of time each morning. It has nothing to do with praying a repetitious appeal once in a 24-hour period for 30 days. Rather it is *one* thing...*one* truth! Above all else, *let your roots grow down into Christ* (Col. 2:7 NLT). The bedrock for us all is the magnificent Savior. If you are going to understand and live this life as a "Christian" you must know the Source. If the passion you feel is going to burn brighter and deeper you *must* let your roots grow down deep into Christ Jesus. This will not happen with a few special minutes of Bible reading each day. It will not occur by reciting a prayer on a daily basis. It will only occur when we see Christ for who He is, recognize the incredible worth of His sacrifice for *us,* and then burst forth with a love that is simply a *response* to what we have seen in the suffering Lamb of Calvary.

Taking a Moment...

Young person, in this moment now as you read these words, take a long-hard look at the cross once more. Forget my crazy stories; blot out distractions around you and let your mind slip back to that cross. When you finish these last few sentences you may want to close this book and just meditate.

Can you see Him? There He is among the soldiers. Can you see the blood-soaked robes? Are you angered as calloused hands strike blows to His head, splitting His cheeks, as blood seeps from His eyes? Do you cringe as razor-edged rocks, on 9 long tails plow up His torso? Does the grisly flesh of His face turn your stomach? Do ribs peeking through His shredded skin bring bile to your throat?

Can you feel the heat of the Jerusalem sun? Do you cry as the hands, which once broke bread for thousands, are severed? What is your reaction when every joint in His frame is ripped from every socket? Do chills run through your body as He whispers forgiveness? Do you tremble as the sky grows black? Do you worship as He screams our triumph?

Let your mind rest upon Him. Remind yourself that nothing else compares to the worth of this one sacrifice. Remind yourself that the Christian life finds its essence, its joy, its pleasure, and its service here. Take as long as you need, young friend.

Find your passion now, from His passion!

Worship Him for forgiveness! Adore Him for His love! Praise Him because He is God!

How do you live a Christian life of passion?

The key my friend is extremely simple: *meditate on the cross, and in so doing, you will fall in love with Christ!*

The Wrong Goal

As an eighth grader who is home schooled, yet plays for a private school's basketball team, you try everything to fit in and grow in popularity. Such was the case for me. A wiry, five foot six inch kid with braces and that shaggy hair, I wasn't the most fashionable guy in the academy. I didn't know what to say, how to dress, when to speak, or—unfortunately in many cases—when *not* to speak. The girls avoided me, and looking back now, I honestly can't blame them.

So you can begin to understand my excitement when I was named the starting point guard of the junior varsity team. I was not quick on the court, as far as foot speed goes, but I was decently smart in my decisions—at least from what I was told—and I had practiced for hours on end to perfect my ball-handling skills. I was proud of the fact that I could break a full-court press, find the open guy, and force coaches to put their best defender on me. That was fun. It was fun hearing parents yell at their kids to get a hand in my face after I had buried another long-ball from three-point land. And if, at this moment, I seem vain, remember that those were my fourteen-year-old glory days, which are long over. Not to mention, if you thought there was another embarrassing story coming out of this...you were right.

The school we were playing will remain nameless. The thing that I will always remember about this particular academy is the horrible hometown officiating. However, we still scraped out wins against this team, and they always played us closely so a rivalry formed between the two schools.

It was one of our earlier encounters, on their home court. It was the second half of the JV game, and naturally, I was running the point. Have you ever had one of those horrid memory failures in a very important instance? Well, I had one such experience that day. We had just come from a time out so perhaps I can blame the error on the break in play. With the score close and the fans screaming, we had the ball to inbound under our own basket. Sadly, I forgot this very significant fact, and racing toward center court I waved my arms wildly calling for the inbound toss. I was open so the ball flew through the air and into my arms. Seeing no one between me and the basket—which happened to be theirs on the other end of the court—I put the ball on the hardwood and raced for the goal!

All I remember was hearing my dad yell, "Aaron, that's the wrong goal!"

I did not make it to the basket. The shrill scream of the referee's whistle brought me to an embarrassing stop, as he indicated a backcourt violation and a turn-over. Completely humiliated, after attempting to score on the other team's hoop, I had to endure the ridicule and mockery of the fans and even my own teammates.

Though it is regrettable to say, the truth is that many young believers are shooting for the wrong goal as well, and as foolish as my error was on the basketball court as an eighth grade boy, the error is far more stupid by Christian youth in the church today!

When I ask college students or teenagers what their goal is in the Christian life I hear a multitude of replies:

"To keep myself clean from the world . . ."

"To stay morally pure . . ."

"To read my Bible at least 30 minutes every day . . ."

"To guard my thought life . . ."

"To have good times of prayer . . ."

"To tell people about the Gospel . . ."

And the list keeps on rolling. Ask a simple question that should have a single, very obvious answer, and you're immediately barraged by dozens, none of them the right one. Sure, morality is important to the Christian, righteous living is needed, Bible study is essential, purity of mind, and a strong prayer life are good things, but, my friend, these should not be our goal.

What should it be? What should be my passion? What should be yours? The answer, my friend, is simple. As we observe the great torture of body and soul that Christ went through for us, the immediate cry from our lips *will* be the cry of one burning passion, *"Lord, I want to know Christ!"*

This is what sets true Christians apart from all others!

This is what ignites our rebellion!

This was the blazing heartbeat of a first-century rebel, the apostle Paul—a man who had gone to the extreme to make himself right with God, a man who without doubt was esteemed by many to be the most notable performer of righteous deeds. He was tremendously advanced in Judaism and passionate about the traditional teaching of his ancestors (Gal. 1:14). This was a man who knew all the ropes of religion, and yet had never found the Person behind and making up all truth. And it was in that dark state of religious evil that God, by a merciful stroke of His sovereign plan, found the young man named Saul and poured out His grace to make this youth a blazing monument to the glory of Christ!

Paul never got over the work of Jesus for his soul. That truth daily transformed his life. If we could walk back through the centuries—with pen in hand and a pad on our knee—and ask the apostle what his goal was, the answer would resound back as recorded in the epistle to the church at Philippi. This would be his "Christian walk" testimony:

> I obeyed the Jewish law so carefully that I was never accused of any fault. I once thought all these things were so very important, but now I consider them worthless because of what Christ has done! Yes, everything else is worthless when compared with the priceless gain of knowing Christ Jesus my Lord. I have discarded everything else, counting it all as garbage, so that I may have Christ and become one with him. I no longer count on my goodness or my ability to obey God's law, but I trust Christ to save me. For God's way of making us right with himself depends on faith. As a result, I can really know Christ (Phil. 3:6–10 NLT).

Does this sound like a man who is *trying* to *dutifully perform* the Christian life? No. Rather this testimony exalts the cross of Christ and screams at us the truth that nothing in all of life can compare with how awesome it is to know the God of gods—Jesus Christ.

Above all else this is what we should long for. This should be our goal. This simple truth should be the bull's eye in the center of the target for us, the redeemed. Righteous living, clean speech, a humble walk, purity of mind—these are all good things, but they are only the spokes in the spinning life that we live. The hub in the center of that life, once again, is Christ! He is our nucleus. Without Him there is no purpose to life, no reason to go on. Truly, if we have the Son, we have *all*.

When I don't feel like it…

Pensacola, Florida, Fall 2003

I won't soon forget moving to Pensacola, Florida. Life was supposed to be exciting there. The beach…three colleges within close proximity to where I lived…a ton of people my age…a lot to do…Boy, was I ever wrong. For weeks on end I struggled through the mundane dealings of every day life.

Searching for a job…working the job…quitting the job…searching for friends…hanging out with my new friends…business plaguing relationships…Yea, life was perplexing for me. Sure, I knew all the right answers to my dilemmas…I knew how I was supposed to live the Christian life. I knew *Who* I was supposed to rely on to carry me through every day…but my gaze was averted. For weeks I labored through the humdrum routine. The cross was not what filled my view. My passion waned, as my vision of the Savior dimmed. Sure, I still read my Bible, had times of prayer, and said that I was depending on Him, but as I began to feel the bite of financial pressure and the weight of every day life without close friends, my faith grew small. I began to depend upon my own strength and intellect…and that got me nowhere.

It was during that time that God brought a friend into my life. She was passionate about life, as I was, and was going through a current struggle as well. We would often talk late at night, discussing the providence of God in jobs, education, relationships, and other "key" issues of importance for young people.

I'll never forget the night it all came to a head for me. I was growing sick of how life was going. Financially things were terrible...emotionally I was empty...but it was my spiritual life that had really begun to stagnate. I was chatting with my friend and we were feeding one another's anxiety when she suddenly spoke a truth that crashed upon me like a ton of cement. At first I shook the statement off, but as God had planned, she repeated the truth. I was outside my apartment, lying on the trunk of my car, gazing heavenward when the precision of her declaration punctured my being and seared my apathetic soul.

Her proclamation was simple, and even now I blush to restate it for it was a thought that I had spoken to teens in difficulty a thousand times before but coming from another's lips it seemed to singe my spirit. Though I cannot recall exactly what she said that evening, and though it was not profound or smooth, I have summed the truth of it up in the statement below:

> *"Whenever we allow circumstances to demoralize our spirit, our satisfaction is resting in something other than God. Whenever we try to rectify those circumstances in our own strength, our pride has minimized the loving control of God."*

Basically, what this truth is teaching is that however we try to deceive ourselves by saying that we are focused on Christ and passionate about Him, the true test will be handed out for us to take through the trials of every day life. You see, when I was living those first few weeks in Pensacola, I claimed to be madly in love with God but my actions revealed clearly that I did not truly believe what He said to be true. I doubted that He would take care of me financially or emotionally, and those areas of my life affected my focus on Christ.

Do things—great or small—get you down? Do you tend to lose hope instead of increasing your faith? Perhaps you are enduring the end of a close relationship. Maybe your best friend just died in a tragic car accident... or your parents are battling through a divorce as you lie neglected on the sidelines. However overwhelming the circumstance is that strikes you with all its ferocity at this moment, I cry out to you as one who has been there many times before...*cast it all on Christ! Keep your eyes on the cross!* This is the key to not just getting through, but to growing strong. Sure, it is easier to say it than live it. It is tough to actually let go...but He will carry you...Hey, rest assured...He *is* carrying you...so let go.

Look constantly to the One who treads out those footprints in the sand for you.

Focus daily on the bloodied hands that bore those nails for *you.*

Breathing it!

If you feebly continue trying to gain the nod of God and increased affection from Him by your works, you will live an insanely frustrated existence. You will forever find yourself in one of two scenarios. Either you will constantly fail to live up to your own expectations and *your "feelings"* will lead you to believe that you are a "pathetic" Christian, or you will succeed in being a victorious Christian in your mind *because* you did what you deemed as necessary to deserve the smile of God. Consequently, you will be living out a life of merit resulting in the pride of the Pharisees. In the end, you will only throw away your life.

Here is the key to ongoing zeal as a rebel for Christ, when you wake up tomorrow morning, look to the cross. Take a time out, press the pause button for at least a brief time, and meditate on Golgotha. Never forget that your life of passion is based upon His passion. Yea, it sounds too simple, but simply try it. Lay all aside for a moment with your Divine Friend. We have been forgiven so much; now our true *Christian* response is to live out of love. Roll out of bed each day with a renewed vigor based not on a demerit system of works, but on a passionate response to extreme grace! Go back to that place you found a few moments ago that place of solitude where you stood facing the twisted body of a dying God.

And, after your mind becomes fixated on Him and as you're basking in the warmth of His Divine presence you will find, my friend, that your life will explode with a holy, zealous passion to know Him, to bathe in His grace, and to breathe His worship!

This is truth. This is passion. This is grace. Depend on it and live as a rebel!

Contact Aaron Currin at
aaron@extreme-grace.org

or order more copies of this book at:

Tate Publishing, LLC

127 East Trade Center Terrace
Mustang, Oklahoma 73064

(888) 361 - 9473

Tate Publishing, Llc
www.tatepublishing.com